# PLANNING A

# SUCCESSFUL

## FUTURE

## Managing to Be Wealthy for Individuals and Their Advisors

# JOHN E. SESTINA

WILEY

Published by John Wiley & Sons, Inc., Hoboken, New Jersey.
Published simultaneously in Canada.

For general information on our other products and services or for technical support, please contact our Customer Care Department within the United States at (800) 762-2974, outside the United States at (317) 572-3993 or fax (317) 572-4002.

Wiley publishes in a variety of print and electronic formats and by print-on-demand. Some material included with standard print versions of this book may not be included in e-books or in print-on-demand. If this book refers to media such as a CD or DVD that is not included in the version you purchased, you may download this material at http://booksupport.wiley.com. For more information about Wiley products, visit www.wiley.com.

*Library of Congress Cataloging-in-Publication Data:*

ISBN 978-1-119-06912-6 (Hardcover)
ISBN 978-1-119-18798-1 (ePDF)
ISBN 978-1-119-18797-4 (ePub)

Cover Design: Wiley
Cover Image: New shoot © zimmytws / iStockphoto

Printed in the United States of America.

10  9  8  7  6  5  4  3  2  1

*To Bobbi and Alison*

# Contents

# Acknowledgments

Thanks to the many clients I have had through the years. They have given me opportunities to see every combination of financial circumstances and improve their financial lives and lifestyles.

I also deeply appreciate the sharing among fellow financial planners, particularly other NAPFA members. We have educated each other as this profession has grown. Special thanks to Margery Wasserman, Bob Underwood, and Jim Schwartz.

Thank you to my contributing authors: Tyler V. Cook, Lawrence Funderburke, Stephen A. Lukan, Bhagwan Satiani, and Kimberly E. Wirtz.

A special thanks to Tula Batanchiev, my editor at John Wiley & Sons, as well as to the other professionals there, including Stacey Rivera. My thanks also to marketing consultant Sandra S. Nichols, who worked with me in the beginning to find creative ways to show consumers that they do indeed have choices in financial planning.

John E. Sestina
Dublin, Ohio

# Preface

If you're a consumer, maybe you wonder why your paycheck never seems to last until the end of the month. Perhaps you've lain awake at night, considering how to pay for your children's college, or tried to make prudent investments, only to see the stock market go down along with your savings.

You're not alone. Most of us struggle to make ends meet, whether we earn an annual $50,000 or $150,000. And when we seek advice, who can understand what the professionals are saying? Finances can be so intimidating! This book will help you chart your way to financial freedom without putting you to sleep or confusing you.

Before you can chart your specific financial plan, however, you need to know the basic concepts behind successful financial planning. Why do you want to invest? What are the obstacles to your financial freedom? Why is it important to start saving now? This book will teach you a proven, tested way to become financially independent. Isn't that what you need? Let your Uncle Harry brag about his latest hot stock tip. You will be able to sit back and smile, knowing that you will achieve your financial goals without any help from Uncle Harry. After all, it's not how much you make along the way, but whether you reach your destination.

If you're a financial planner, this book offers you a look inside the thinking of one of the country's preeminent financial planners. I began building and refining my wealth management system in 1965. In this book, I cover everything from the philosophical advantages of fee-only planning to tips on what clients should expect from you and how you can best serve their needs.

When I taught the first university-level course in personal financial planning in 1969, few had even heard the term. No one could have predicted that fee-only financial planning would be so popular nearly 50 years later.

- Consistent processes, designations, and organizations have helped make financial planning a profession.
- The National Association of Personal Financial Advisors (NAPFA), made up exclusively of fee-only financial planners, has grown from 60 members at its beginning to a global organization with more than 2,400 members
- Financial planners can earn 21 different professional designations in more than 20 job titles dealing with different aspects of the field. Colleges and universities in nearly every state prepare students for the profession.
- Financial planning has grown to the extent that it warrants government regulation from both federal and state oversight bodies.
- Countless websites market the services of industry participants seeking to capitalize on the growing popularity of personal financial planning.

Establishing a brand-new profession has been a long, challenging, and rewarding road.

When I started looking for my first client in 1965, financial compensation was a concern. By the early 1970s, I had run the compensation gamut. I had taken commissions only, charged fees and taken commissions, and charged fees and offset them with commissions. I felt compelled to make a decision. Charging fees and accepting commissions from product sales had too much potential for clouding my recommendations. Offering the optimum in nonbiased advice required that I charge fees only.

About that time, I learned that another planner had become successful by charging fees rather than selling products. I met with him and soon discovered a few others who had the same philosophical concerns that I did. Out of that core group grew the fee-only financial planning movement and the first national fee-only organization, the National

Association of Personal Financial Advisors (NAPFA), which I founded with Bob Underwood and Jim Schwartz.

Fee-only financial planning is a client-centered, profitable profession. My experience has proved that an educated, motivated entrepreneur can become wealthy in his or her own right. The system is simple: give your clients the objectivity, comprehensiveness, and peace of mind they want. Financial planning must be client-centered in order to be profitable.

In the early years, a common misconception held that only the very wealthy could afford the best in objective and comprehensive advice. In truth, fee-only financial planning can be accessible to everyone.

Fee-only planners have the opportunity to serve an enormous and largely untapped market. Today's consumers are both more affluent and more educated than in the past. Thanks also to the technology revolution, they can become much more personally engaged in the planning process. Working with educated and involved clients is always more productive and profitable for both parties.

Making fee-only financial planning accessible on a systematic basis to every American was the foundation for creating the Sestina Network of Fee-Only Financial Planners in 1994. Others have also seen the potential and are following suit.

This book systematizes a wealth of resources to support your success in fee-only financial planning.

# Introduction

No matter how dire your situation, there is hope. You can take control of your financial life and build a prosperous future.

I'm saying this from personal experience. I was raised in a coal camp near Clarksburg, West Virginia, the son of an uneducated miner. The tarpaper shack I called home had no running water. I lost the first joint of a finger when I played catch with a sharp piece of anthracite, a common pastime in a setting with few childhood diversions. My parents had no way to help me get an education or any start toward a prosperous adult life. I have faced poverty, disconnected utilities, empty refrigerators, and thieving business partners.

I am also the well-educated, prosperous owner of a financial planning firm, a loving husband, and a devoted father. I've earned the ability to enjoy my friends, my hobbies, my family, and the financial security I've created. I did it myself, and I am absolutely passionate about helping you do it, too.

This book is the culmination of my career as a financial planner. In it, I endeavor to share decades of knowledge and experience in both the nuts and bolts of planning and investing, which you can find in other places, and my thinking about money and life, which you will only find here.

At its best, I believe that good financial planning is synergistic. When you learn to set and achieve financial goals, you also learn a great deal about yourself: your priorities, your values, your beliefs about marriage and family, your professional ideals. When we align money with our deepest beliefs, we become much more able to lead lives that are in keeping with our values.

In that sense, this book is only partially about money. At a deeper level, it is about teaching you to find and bring out the best in yourself. Whether you're 26 and have tons of student debt, 40 and realizing that you will have two kids in college at the same time, or 60 and worried about retiring, there is help and hope for you.

Reacting to financial circumstances is what most people do. Retirement is five years away, and they wonder how they'll have enough money to live on, never mind enough money to travel to places they've always dreamed of going. Their child is due to begin college in just three years. How will they get the money they need to pay tuition and other college expenses? Or perhaps they hear about what someone else calls a great investment opportunity. How do they know whether it's a wonderful opportunity for *them*?

So many of us wait until the need for money or decisions is nearly upon us before we take action. It can be different for you. In this book, I will show you—as I've shown clients for 50 years—how you can achieve financial independence by making financial decisions proactively, not reactively. You have the ability to take care of yourself and your family, without waiting for any kind of miracle. I'll show you how.

## Creating Your Financial Plan

The key is in creating a financial plan. An individual financial plan is a map, helping you navigate the complex, constantly changing world of finance. This book will guide you as you prepare your plan and put it into action. That will take time and effort, but it will also help you sleep better at night, undisturbed by worries and questions about money.

This book will help you create your own financial plan and will also tell you what a financial planner can do for you, how to find a good planner, and how to best work with that person when your search is successful. If you're a planner, it's my hope that this book will serve as a kind of mentor, showing you my thinking on a variety of issues, including what good financial planning entails.

If you already have insurance, an estate plan, investments, tax planning, a college fund, or a pension, you might think that your financial plan is already set. Think again. What you have isn't a financial plan. A good financial plan incorporates everything you already have and adds an objective evaluation of your current financial picture, your goals, and what it will take for you to achieve those goals. Pull all these things together in an organized way, and you have a financial plan.

A financial plan helps you understand what you have now, where you want to be, and how you will get there. It's personal, designed to map an individual path between your current position and your unique end goal. It's not your neighbor's retirement plan or one created by a computer algorithm.

Follow the lessons in this book, and you will learn to manage your money and your life so that eventually you can attain financial independence. Working will be an option for you—not a requirement.

## How Does This Relate to Investing?

Financial planning is more than investing. Many people believe that choosing the right investments will put them on the proverbial Easy Street. But this isn't usually the way things work out. Most people react to each financial event, instead of planning ahead for their whole financial future. When they hear a hot stock tip, they buy stocks. When they hear gold is going up, they buy gold. But they never consider which investments will help them achieve financial freedom and when and how to buy. You will learn a step-by-step process for setting up an investing plan, as well as how to avoid common investment mistakes.

## Are You Meeting Your Goals?

Throughout this book, I explode some myths about money, taxes, insurance, and investments, reminding you that taxes, rates of return, and other details are just that: details. It's easy to let them become short-term distractions from your long-term goal. You don't win this game by paying the least in taxes or getting the best return on your investments. You win by reaching your goal.

Let's say your goal is to save $1 million in the next 10 years. The first year, you put $100,000 in your savings account. The second year, you put $100,000 under the mattress. The third year, you hide $100,000 in the closet. Every year for 10 years, you put aside $100,000. At the end of 10 years, you've met your goal—and where you stashed the money, how much return you earned on it, or what taxes you paid on it don't matter very much.

Working through the financial planning process helps you find the money you need to meet your goals. When you have both goals and a financial plan, you will know when:

- You don't have enough money, and you must revise your goal or reach it later than you'd hoped.

- Or you have enough or more than enough money and can reach your goal on time or sooner than you'd planned.

You may not like what you discover. Your goals may have to change. But you'll know where you stand—and where you stand may be within reach of surprisingly high achievements.

## Obstacles to Reaching Financial Goals

Along the way, you'll learn more about the obstacles that prevent many people from reaching their financial goals: taxes, inflation, death and disability, lack of a plan, ego, and leakage.

Federal and state taxes are said to be one of life's two certainties, and they're nearly always on the rise. Fortunately, there are ways to minimize the taxes you pay.

Inflation eats away at income. Those who don't plan for it can end up with less than they need. Inflation is one of the villains that can get people into financial trouble before they realize it. Even a tiny amount of inflation over time can affect your lifestyle if you don't plan properly. Consistent planning and saving can help you stay ahead of inflation.

Although no one likes to talk about them, death and disability can be devastating to a family that has not planned for these events. You may have estate plans, and you should have a will. Alone, however, these are not enough. What would your financial situation be if a disability forced you to stop work for months, years, or perhaps the rest of your life?

How would you cope as you watch your car being repossessed? How would you feel if your spouse had to work two jobs? Many find it uncomfortable or even painful to talk or think about these things, but you must. You will learn how to plan for death and disability, giving you a greater sense of security than you have now.

I've already mentioned that many people react to financial events as they happen, instead of creating a unified plan for reaching their goals. Without a plan, you'll have a much lower chance of success.

Ego is the hardest obstacle to overcome. Some people cannot reach their financial goals because their egos get in the way. They buy cars and join clubs to impress people. They live in houses they can't afford. Instead of planning for the future, they keep up with the Joneses today, a decision that keeps them from reaching financial independence. I'll show you what happens if you increase your lifestyle one year too soon. You'll be shocked by the difference one year can make in whether you reach your goals.

Leakage can be a hidden obstacle between you and your financial goals. Leakage happens when you don't reinvest your investment earnings to help you meet your goal. Did you spend your last stock dividend, instead of investing it? That's leakage, and it can really add up over time. If you save $5,000 a year and earn 10 percent annually, you would earn $500 the first year. It's so easy to spend that 500 on immediate needs and wants. If you do that, after 20 years you will have the money you put in: $100,000. But if you reinvest the interest every year, you'll have $286,375 instead. Are those new clothes or golf clubs worth a difference of more than $186,000?

Leakage also occurs when you pick an arbitrary dollar amount as a goal, but sabotage your goal by spending part of that money. For example, you think things would be great if you had $30,000. When you've saved $30,000, you celebrate with a vacation that costs

$5,000, leaving you with just $25,000. You can build back to $30,000, but a lack of discipline has cost you time and compound interest. To avoid leakage, you must treat the money you are saving and investing as untouchable for any purpose other than your goal. Otherwise, you erode your nest egg. Don't spend the college savings on a new car.

## Fuel Your Goals with Income

You know that a financial plan is your road map to financial freedom, and you've seen some of the obstacles in the road ahead. What fuel will get you to your goal? You'll need financial gasoline in the form of your earnings.

The next sentence is one of the most important you'll read in any book about personal finance: **whatever your earnings are, they are**. They aren't any bigger and they aren't any smaller. You must find a way to live within your current financial means.

You can't live now on what you think the future will bring. Maybe you'll get a raise or a bonus next year, or perhaps your business has good prospects. That's great—for the future. It means nothing right now.

It's surprising how many people don't know what they earn, especially if their pay is hourly, seasonal, or includes sporadic bonuses. Nor do they know what they spend, because they don't keep track of their purchases. To make a financial plan, you need to know how much money you need to fund your current lifestyle. If you're married, your spouse must also know how much money comes in and how much goes out in any given month, so you can act as a team.

Communication is key. In many couples, one spouse—often the husband—handles the family finances. When he dies, his wife doesn't know the lawyer or the accountant, isn't aware of the trust fund, and struggles to understand her finances while grieving at the same time. You might think it's difficult to talk about financial matters now.

How difficult will it be for your family to begin a steep financial learning curve the week after your death?

## Developing Your Plan

You will get as much out of this book as you put into it. Don't be intimidated. I will walk you through every step of building your financial plan.

If you make less than $50,000 a year, this book contains the tools you need to prepare your financial plan. If you earn more than $50,000 a year, this book can still help you complete the basics of your financial plan, giving you the structure and questions you'll need to make the best use of your time with a financial planner.

After you have a financial plan, it will take only a few hours each week to manage it. Anyone can learn to manage money, even with a busy schedule—though you may need to overcome the most common obstacles to doing so.

Maybe you don't understand the language financial experts use. I will explain the concepts so that you can understand fully, ask intelligent questions, and become an active participant in your own financial life.

Or perhaps you've always let your spouse, your stockbroker, or a relative manage your finances. Isn't it time that you understand your financial situation? It doesn't have to be a mystifying process, even though many financial advisers may want you to think that.

Do finances sound complicated? They are, but not because you're stupid. Finances are inherently complex. The markets are constantly changing. Just trying to figure out the implications of each new tax law generates hundreds of billable hours for attorneys and accountants. People who work in finance must continually read and study, just to keep up.

The subject doesn't have to confuse you. I will explain things in everyday terms. By the time you finish this book, you will be able to prepare your first financial plan.

## Attaining Peace of Mind

The ultimate products of financial planning are financial independence and peace of mind. Once you get a good financial plan, the pressure comes off. You know your goals, how you are working toward them, and where you are on that journey.

Ready to begin? Let's explore together.

## Summary

No matter what your situation, there is help and hope for you.

Most people react to financial situations. They should be planning for them instead.

Everyone needs a financial plan. Plans help you navigate the complex, constantly changing financial world. They help you control your money, rather than letting your money control you.

A financial plan is not just insurance, investments, investing, or tax planning. A good financial plan is a combination of these, plus an objective evaluation of where you are now, what you want, when you want it, and what it will take to reach your goals.

Whatever your earnings are, they are—no more, no less. Learn to live within your current means.

# CHAPTER 1

# What Do You Want?

When you dream, what do you dream about? Do you want to tour Europe or go fishing when you retire? Would you like your children to go to Harvard or to a state university? Do you want to leave millions to your favorite charity or give your stamp collection to your favorite nephew?

We all have different dreams, unique wish lists of what we want for ourselves and our families, for now and for later. In this chapter, I'll help you put your goals in writing, perhaps for the first time. Don't let my questions restrict you. If you want something that I haven't mentioned, write it down. This is your wish list.

Don't be afraid to dream big. We'll discuss the realities of how you'll get there. For now, focus on your wishes.

## Put It in Writing

You're a busy person. Why take the time to write down things that you already know?

- Writing down your dreams is the first step toward making them a reality. By putting words on paper, you turn dreams into goals. That's why you should be as specific as possible. Don't write, "I want to retire with lots of money." Define "lots of money" by assigning your goal a dollar amount: "I want to have an annual income of $50,000 in today's dollars when I retire." Or list the things you'd like to do and the lifestyle you want to have, then assign a dollar value.

- Writing down your dreams brings to light any information gaps. How much insurance do you have? Where are your policies? What are the total annual costs today at the college your child might attend?

- Writing down your dreams and sharing them with your family opens communication and can keep everyone focused on the same goals. You may already have discussed your hopes for the future with your family. If not, you may be surprised to discover that your family members have goals that are different from yours. What if your spouse wants to retire near the ocean, far from your beloved mountains? It's better to discuss these things now than be unpleasantly surprised later.

- Writing down your dreams and informing your advisors helps them serve you better. The more they know about what you want, the more they can tailor their services to your specific needs. If you don't want to leave a large estate, for instance, your insurance agent shouldn't try to sell you extra life insurance. If you want your spouse to continue your business if you die first, your attorney should include that in your will and go over the paperwork with both partners.

- Writing down and regularly reviewing your dreams helps keep your goals current—and your other details up-to-date as well. Have you had more children since you last updated your wish list? Have some of your children become adults since you considered your overall financial affairs? Are your will and insurance coverage up to date? None of us is the same person today that we were five years ago. Our dreams change. Our financial plan should keep up, so those dreams can become reality.

## Six Steps to Financial Freedom

Now that you've written down your financial wish list, it's time to introduce the six steps you'll use in preparing your financial plan. Working through these steps and using the explanations and advice in this book will put you on your way to financial independence.

That might sound complicated, but it's not. In fact, the steps may seem familiar. You follow a similar planning process every day without realizing it, whether you're painting the house or cooking a meal. Here are the six steps and two simple examples to show how they work.

**Planning Process**

1. What do you want? Identify your goal.

2. What do you have now? Collect information.

3. What's holding you back? Consider the obstacles standing between you and your goal. Brainstorm alternate solutions and ways to remove or work around your obstacles.

4. How can you get what you want? Develop written recommendations.

5. Choose a plan and put it into action.

6. Is your plan working? Review your goal and strategies for reaching it at least once a year.

   You use the same steps to paint a house:

1. Identify your goal. Spruce up the house with a new coat of paint.

2. Collect information. How many square feet need to be painted? Are there any spots that need primer? How many square feet?

3. Consider the obstacles between you and your goal. Perhaps you don't like painting houses, or don't have time to do the job.

4. Brainstorm possible solutions. You could put on primer, then paint. You could also paint next year, hire someone else to do the work, or install siding.

5. You choose the first option. Overcome your distaste for the job. You buy primer, put it on, and then paint the house.

6. The house looks great! Six months later, it still looks good. Pat yourself on the back.

   The same process works as you prepare a meal:

1. Your goal. Prepare lunch for four people.

2. Gather information. What ingredients do you have?

**3.** Identify obstacles. You have only one pound of ground beef.

**4.** Brainstorm potential solutions. You could make small hamburgers and add side dishes to complete the meal, go to the store and buy more ground beef, make something else with the ingredients you have on hand, or go out for lunch.

**5.** You go out to eat.

**6.** Lunch was not that good. You might decide to go out for lunch again but at a different restaurant.

Obviously, preparing your financial plan will take a little more thought. Here is a description of each of the financial planning steps and how they will help you build your financial plan.

**1.** By now, you know that you should write down your goals.

**2.** What do you have now?

Collect information in the form of all your important financial data. Finding these documents may be a treasure hunt, and doing a thorough job will probably take some time. The following chapter has a document checklist, to ensure that you don't miss anything.

**3.** What's holding you back?

Consider the problem areas in your finances. What is preventing you from achieving financial independence? You probably have struggled with one or more of these common problems:

- High taxes
- Too little or too much insurance
- Inadequate cash flow
- Poor liquidity
- High debt
- Low rate of return

This book will help you tackle these problems and find workable solutions.

**4.** How will you get what you want?

After you've documented your wishes and know what you have now, you must analyze your situation and develop specific ways to meet your financial goals. If your investment rate of return is too low to meet your goals, for instance, you might want to raise your rate of return. This book will teach you several ways to do that.

**5.** Put Your Plan into Action

A good financial plan only works if you put it into action. If you want to raise your rate of return on investments, to continue the previous example, you must choose a particular investment that meets your need for a better return and then invest in it.

That sounds simple, but isn't for everyone. Many people are great at planning but put off taking action. (Others want to take action immediately, without putting a plan into place.)

**6.** Review the plan. Is it working?

No financial plan should be carved in stone. Review it annually, being honest with yourself, your spouse, and your financial planner. You should also review your plan and its execution in unusual circumstances: a birth or a death in the family, an inheritance, a substantial professional shift, or a significant change in your or your spouse's health.

## Start Planning

Now that you understand the planning process, let's get started. Get out a pencil and at least five sheets of paper. Label the five sheets with the following headings:

**1.** Retirement plan

**2.** Education plan

**3.** Estate plan

**4.** Disability plan

**5.** Other needs

Here are some questions to get you started in each area. Remember to be as specific as you can. However, if you don't know how much something will cost, put down a guess and go on. Don't get too bogged down in details at this point. Later on you will fill in more details about each wish.

**Your Retirement Plan**

**1.** How old are you now and at what age do you want to retire? How about your spouse? You may want to retire at 40, but realistically expect to retire at 55. Go ahead and write down both numbers. As you prepare your financial plan, you will find out which age is better for you. (Do you think you're too young to be planning your retirement? If you're 21, prepare your plan according to the steps in this book, and put that plan into action, you probably can retire at age 40. It's never too early or too late to start your financial plan. Any planning for retirement, even if you have just retired, is better than no financial planning.)

**2.** Do you want to retire all at once or gradually cut back your work hours? If you retire from one job, do you plan to start a business or work at a different job but for fewer hours? Will you earn more, less, or the same income? Do you plan to live at least in part on your income, or prefer to live on investments, pensions, and Social Security?

Remember that retirement doesn't have to mean rocking chairs. I know many retired people who put in full days managing their own money or continuing to work at what they enjoy. You don't have to put yourself in mothballs just because you retire.

**3.** How much money will you need to maintain your desired standard of living? No one has a crystal ball, so this isn't an easy question to answer. For now, use this simple equation to estimate your costs:

**Costs that will increase, plus the most money you might need, minus costs that may be eliminated or reduced, equals the least money you might need.**

For example, if you plan to retire to a warm state and spend most of your time there, the amount you spend on heating and winter clothes will be reduced or eliminated. Air conditioning costs may be more than you currently pay. Because you are getting older, your health costs will eventually increase. Depending on your health insurance arrangements, you may need to add a large amount to your needs estimate to cover increased health costs.

You can beat inflation. In the chapter on investing, you will learn specific ways to make your investments grow faster than inflation. These techniques mean that you can estimate your retirement costs in today's dollars. Your money should have the same purchasing power, even years later.

4. How many years of retirement do you need to fund? Ideally, of course, you'd drop dead at a ripe old age, right after you spend your last nickel. To get a sense of how long from now that might be, use an insurance industry life expectancy table. Obviously, if your grand-parents and parents all lived to 100, then you may want to add a few more years to your life estimate and congratulate yourself on picking the right ancestors.

5. What do you want to do when you retire? You may want to continue your life just as it is today, or you may plan some drastic changes. Maybe you're in between. Whatever you've dreamed of doing in retirement, write it down and consider taking the first steps toward making it a reality. If you want to paint but have never picked up a brush, take a beginning art course. You might love it, or you might be allergic to paint.

**Your Education Plan**

1. How many children will you send to college? This question is more difficult than it may seem. You may hope your children become doctors or lawyers, but they may become plumbers (and probably make more money). If your children are young, college decisions are far in the future. For now, assume they will go and plan accordingly.

Do you want to return to college? Add yourself to your education plan.

2. What are your children's current ages? Will more than one attend college at a time?

3. How many years until your children start college? List years to enrollment for each child.

4. How many years will they attend college? There are two-year and four-year schools, graduate schools, and professional schools. How many years do you want to fund?

5. What is the current cost of college? Choose one or more possible colleges and find out the current cost for one year of tuition, room and board, books, lab fees, and personal expenses.

What is the rate of increase for tuition? At present, college tuitions increase faster than the current rate of inflation. Keep an eye on these increases as you reevaluate your financial plan each year.

What are the possibilities for scholarships, grants, and other financial aid? Obviously, you'll have a better sense of this for older children. Have you looked into these ways of paying for college? Do you want to consider them? Many colleges let visitors use a website calculator to get a rough estimate of the need-based aid they might receive.

**Your Estate Plan**

1. Do you have a current will? Does your spouse?

2. What if you die first? How much you want to leave for your family may depend on whether your spouse works outside the home (and would continue doing so) and the ages of your children, if any.

3. If you were a full-time homemaker, what services, such as housekeeping, driving, childcare, cooking, and home management, would your family have to replace? If you work outside the home, what income, insurance, or other benefits would your family need to replace?

4.  What if both of you die at the same time? What do you want to do with your estate?

5.  Would your estate need to pay bills, mortgages, or business obligations?

6.  How much money would your family need right away to handle day-to-day expenses? How long does it take an estate to be probated in your area? Will any other bills come due during this time?

7.  Do you need a dedicated college fund? Look again at your education plan in light of your estate plan.

8.  If you or your spouse dies, would the survivor want to sell the house immediately or stay there for at least a year?

9.  Do you want to leave anything to family, friends, charities, or other organizations?

10. Will your estate include money, real estate, and/or personal property?

11. Who will get what? Do you want to divide things equally? Do you want to give percentages? Do you want to specify priorities for the distribution of your estate or direct that someone get a minimum amount, in case your estate is worth less than you anticipated?

12. Does any bequest come with conditions? Do you want to give a lump sum, a certain amount each year, or a bequest made only if certain requirements are met?

13. Do you want to exclude someone specifically?

### Your Disability Plan

1.  What happens if you cannot work and have no income? What will you do if your income stops for a short time (less than two years), for more than two years, or for the rest of your life (permanent disability)? Where would you get money to live on?

2.  What happens if your spouse's income disappears? Consider the same three scenarios.

**3.** What costs could you eliminate or defer for any of these scenarios? Do you have insurance to cover lost wages?

**4.** What percent of your current income could you live on in any of these scenarios? If you had to make do with a minimum sum, would you need 80 percent of your current income? 100 percent? More? Some people could tighten their belts and get by. Others might need more than their current income if their medical insurance did not cover the costs of the disability. What would be right for you?

## Other Goals

In addition to our basic needs, we all have other goals we would like to reach. Maybe you want a bigger house, a new car every three years, or a vacation every six months. Write down these goals.

We all need to plan for the future and its uncertainties, but it's important to maintain a healthy balance between tomorrow and today. After all, you live in the here and now. When you follow a good financial plan, you can enjoy today more, knowing that you've planned for the future.

## Review Your Plans with Your Family Members and Advisors

Sometimes this is the hardest part. You may find out you and your spouse have very different goals. It's better to know this now. Couples should agree on the general direction of their goals. If you and your partner have different goals, consider whether it's possible to attain both. After all, if I want a vacation every six months and you want a new car every three years, we may be able to make everyone happy. But if you want to leave our estate to our children and I want to leave it to charity, we have a problem. Talk honestly about your hopes and dreams until you resolve your conflicts. A financial planner can't help you reach conflicting goals.

On the other hand, you may be pleasantly surprised to discover that both of you have always wanted to try your hand at painting, but somehow it never came up in your conversations.

Discussing your plan with family members may uncover overlooked items. Perhaps a special relative should be included in your estate planning, for instance. You may want to discuss your plan with your children as well as your spouse, to explain the reasoning behind your decisions and eliminate any unpleasant surprises.

It's common sense to share your thoughts with your financial advisor, too. An advisor can only help you reach the goals that you reveal—and can be a valuable partner in ensuring that your strategies are in line with those goals. You may have instructed your stockbroker to invest conservatively. Does that fit with the dreams you've listed, or do you need to take a more aggressive stance? If you want to leave an estate of $5 million, then you may need to make your insurance dollars work harder for you by buying more term insurance instead of whole life.

## You Know What You Want

As we've seen, a financial plan must start with a list of what you want. Before you go on to the next chapter, review what you've written on your five sheets of paper. You may want to adjust one set of plans in light of the others. These are your goals; revise them until they are right for you and your family.

Now it's time to add more substance to those dreams by filling in the details. We'll do that in the next chapter.

## Summary

1. What do you want out of life? You must write down your goals in order to achieve them, find information gaps, let your family know what you want, and help your advisors serve you better.

2. There are six steps to financial freedom. To prepare your financial plan, you and your spouse should work through each step.

3. Review your plan with your financial advisors. Consider their suggestions, but make the final decisions with your spouse.

# CHAPTER 2

# What Do You Have Now?

**D**o you know your net worth? Do you know your total debt? Do you have a rough idea of how much you'll owe in taxes this year?

If you answered yes to all these questions, then you probably have your financial information well organized—and you will breeze through this chapter. However, most of us have only a vague idea of the answers to these and other questions about our financial data. This chapter may take effort, but it will be rewarding to finally know the answers.

In this chapter, you will work through a checklist of the financial information you must find. You may discover that you're missing some data, and you'll need to fill in those gaps.

Next, you'll do cash flow planning, which includes using your spendable cash worksheet to estimate the taxes that you'll owe this year. The spendable cash worksheet will also give you the benchmark data you need to analyze new financial proposals.

Finally, you'll create a balance sheet, which will tell you your bottom line: how much your assets are worth, right now. When you review your financial plan next year, you'll see how much you've gained or lost.

Why all the bother? You need to know what you have now. Memory is unreliable, so the only way to know for sure is to get out your financial papers.

How long will it take to work through this chapter? A lot depends on the complexity of your financial affairs. If you're single with few investments, then a few hours may be enough. If you're married with children, have many investments, own your own business, and/or have complex estate plans, it will take longer. Allow time to review the results of this chapter's work with your spouse and financial advisor, if you are working with one. They may catch items you missed. Don't get discouraged! Planning for your future is a lot easier than not having a plan for your future.

## Materials

You'll need a few materials to help you get organized

- A financial calculator
- At least 16 file folders, to start
- An accordion file
- A 13-column ruled accountant's pad for your cash flow worksheet

You can do the necessary calculations with an ordinary calculator or by using the web links we suggest. However, it's easier to calculate percentages and other results with a financial calculator. If you have a computer, a spreadsheet program will help you keep track of all these details.

## Information You'll Need

Figure 2.1 shows the financial information you must collect and put into your folders. If an item doesn't apply to you, go on to the next item. You may not need a folder for every item on this list. In fact, you may wish to start with the 16 main headings listed so you don't get overwhelmed. For some items, such as general insurance, you may need a folder for each type of policy.

## Filing the Information

Look at your paperwork as you find and file it. Does your memory match the printed document? Make a note to change anything that needs adjusting at this point. For example, you may think that an account is jointly owned when it is not. There are significant consequences to your estate plan if the ownership is not correct for the plan you are creating.

Obviously, all this information is valuable to you, so keep it in a safe place. If you have actual stock or bond certificates, put copies of

FIGURE 2.1

# Information You Need for Your Financial Plan

1. Cash equivalents (checking and savings accounts)
2. Stocks and mutual funds
3. Bonds
4. Oil, gas, mineral investments or rights, commodities, arbitrage, venture capital, gold, collectibles, artwork, jewelry
5. Real estate
    Residence
    Investment
    Real estate investment trust (REIT) holdings
6. Receivables
7. Business interests
    Employment agreement
    Medical/dental agreement
    Buys/sell agreement
    Partnership agreement
    Corporate tax returns (1120)
8. Liabilities
    Mortgages
    Installment loans
    Credit cards
    Leases
9. Life insurance
10. Health and accident insurance
    Hospitalization/major medical
    Expense reimbursement
    Disability
11. General insurance
    Homeowners' property comprehensive policy
    Automobile insurance
    Office insurance
    Professional liability insurance
    Umbrella insurance
    Fidelity
    Marine

*(Continued)*

---

**FIGURE 2.1**

# Information You Need for Your Financial Plan (continued)

**12.** Estate planning
- Wills
- Trusts
- Powers of attorney
- Legal documents

**13.** Retirement planning
- Defined-contribution pension
- Defined-benefit pension
- Profit sharing
- Keogh
- IRA
- 401(k)
- Public employee retirement system
- State teacher retirement system

**14.** Education planning

**15.** Income planning
- Personal tax returns (1040)

**16.** Miscellaneous

---

them in the proper folder. Put the originals in your safe deposit box. If a broker holds your stock and/or bond certificates, put the latest brokerage statement in the folder.

Keep the information together until you have completed your financial plan. You'll need to refer back to various items as you work through the rest of this book. Keeping the papers organized and handy helps you keep your momentum.

## Looking for Missing Financial Information

Were you able to find every piece of information? Most of us come up a little short. If it's not where you thought you left it, try:

Safe deposit box

Safe (office and home)

Stockbroker

Family attorney

Tax attorney

Insurance agent

Accountant

File cabinet at work

Your briefcase or purse

Desk at home

File cabinet at home

Kitchen drawer

Dresser drawer

On top of high bookshelves or cabinets

Behind or in books on bookshelves

Underneath the mattress, furniture, or floorboards

Shoeboxes

Closets

Basement, attic, or other storage places

You may smile at some of these locations, but people do put things in the strangest places. Do you have a favorite secret storage place of your own? Check it. Sometimes we put things in temporary safe places until we can get to the safe deposit box or other permanent storage place. Then we forget and that temporary place becomes permanent.

Still can't find the missing paper? It's time to get the document replaced. You can get a duplicate of nearly any document, from birth certificate to bonds, if you have some other proof of ownership or can provide specific information about the item. Use the phone, write a letter, or make a visit. Take the time now to document the information you need.

## Understand What You Have

As you retrieve and sort your financial papers, it's vitally important that you read them. You may find that all is in order—or that the papers contain errors you must correct or spark questions that require answers.

I have a client who owns three convenience stores with his brother. One store has no debt and pays nothing to lease the land on which it stands. The second store pays rent for the land it occupies, and the third store has an enormous mortgage. There is no written agreement between the brothers, and no indication of whether their ownership is joint, several, or nonrecourse. My client is personally liable for at least some of the debt but isn't sure whether he is also liable for his brother's portion, if his brother is unable or unwilling to pay. These are all questions that we need to clear up as part of creating his financial plan.

Another client showed me a life insurance policy that included a wrong birth date. That would jeopardize a future claim, so we moved to correct it immediately.

A third client had two life insurance policies, one for his children and the other to benefit his longtime girlfriend. When the insurance company discovered that he hadn't disclosed a felony arrest in the distant past, they refused to pay the death benefit on either policy.

Give your financial documents a high level of scrutiny. As in these cases, small mistakes can carry serious consequences.

## Cash Flow Planning: When, Where, and How Much?

Now that your information is assembled, it's time to begin the worksheets. Use the blank worksheet in Figures 2.2. Read through the following descriptions of how to fill in each worksheet, and then get to work.

### Cash Flow Worksheet

Complete the cash flow worksheet first. It shows how much income you have and how much money you actually spend in any given month. The worksheet will clearly pinpoint your cash flow problems and show you where money may be idling in your checking account, earning little or no interest. Information from this worksheet also goes into other worksheets.

This isn't a budget. Budgets are destined to fail, because they don't properly prepare you for regular expenses. If you begin budgeting in

FIGURE 2.2

## Blank Worksheet

| SAMPLE | MAR | APR | MAY | JUN | JUL | AUG | SEP | OCT | NOV | DEC | JAN | FEB | TOTALS |
|---|---|---|---|---|---|---|---|---|---|---|---|---|---|
| 1 Cash available INCOME | | | | | | | | | | | | | |
| 2 Salary | | | | | | | | | | | | | |
| 3 Self-employment net income | | | | | | | | | | | | | |
| 4 Investment income | | | | | | | | | | | | | |
| 5 TOTAL INCOME | | | | | | | | | | | | | |
| 6 TOTAL CASH EXPENSES | | | | | | | | | | | | | |
| 7 Taxes—personal property | | | | | | | | | | | | | |
| 8 Taxes—real estate | | | | | | | | | | | | | |
| 9 Home maintenance | | | | | | | | | | | | | |
| 10 Food | | | | | | | | | | | | | |
| 11 Household expenses | | | | | | | | | | | | | |

(Continued)

**FIGURE 2.2**

# Blank Worksheet (continued)

| SAMPLE | MAR | APR | MAY | JUN | JUL | AUG | SEP | OCT | NOV | DEC | JAN | FEB | TOTALS |
|---|---|---|---|---|---|---|---|---|---|---|---|---|---|
| 12 Medical/dental | | | | | | | | | | | | | |
| 13 Clothes | | | | | | | | | | | | | |
| 14 Charitable contributions | | | | | | | | | | | | | |
| 15 Auto—gas/repairs | | | | | | | | | | | | | |
| 16 Home mortgage | | | | | | | | | | | | | |
| 17 Telephone—home | | | | | | | | | | | | | |
| 18 Electric—home | | | | | | | | | | | | | |
| 19 Water—home | | | | | | | | | | | | | |
| 20 Cable—home | | | | | | | | | | | | | |
| 21 Business expense | | | | | | | | | | | | | |
| 22 Education | | | | | | | | | | | | | |
| 23 Insurance—life | | | | | | | | | | | | | |

| # | Item |
|---|------|
| 24 | Insurance—home |
| 25 | Insurance—car |
| 26 | Insurance—personal umbrella |
| 27 | Gifts |
| 28 | Vacations |
| 29 | Miscellaneous |
| 30 | Lessons |
| 31 | Camp |
| 32 | Bank loan #1 |
| 33 | Bank loan #2 |
| 34 | Bank loan #3 |
| 35 | Bank loan #4 |
| 36 | TOTAL EXPENSES |
| 37 | NET INCOME |
| 38 | CUMULATIVE SURPLUS |

April for instance and plan to spend $500 a month on insurance, what are you to do when the quarterly insurance bill for $1,500 comes due in May? In a cash flow worksheet, you note the actual amounts you spend each month—the $1,500 check you write to an insurance company in May—not estimated amounts, or the $500 a month you might budget for that expense.

Figure 2.3 shows an example of a cash flow worksheet. Each month has a column, and each row (income or expense item) should have a number in each month's column. (These numbers just illustrate the concept. Please don't use them as guides to what you should be spending!)

At the bottom, we calculate total expenses and net income. In this case, there is a cumulative surplus. Note that negative numbers are shown in parentheses (see April's net income figure at the bottom of the worksheet). This is a common accounting practice.

The categories on the left side of the worksheet show you what's necessary. "Cash available" is liquid cash: what you could get tomorrow morning from your savings or other cash accounts. Use this for the first month you fill out the worksheet. For subsequent months, your cash available is the "cumulative surplus" amount at the bottom of the worksheet. "Salary" is shown on your pay stubs.

## Income

Some people think a cash flow worksheet is only for those who earn a salary. Not true. The exercise is even more important for those with variable incomes, who have a particularly pressing need to manage their cash flow. The key is to set and work toward a particular income goal.

If you receive dividends or interest, you should know when they are paid.

That's the "income" part of the worksheet.

## Expenses

You'll need many rows to list your expenses. You may have more or fewer than the example, which can help you think of all possible expenses.

FIGURE 2.3

# Sample Cash Flow Worksheet

| SAMPLE | MAR | APR | MAY | JUN | JUL | AUG | SEP | OCT | NOV | DEC | JAN | FEB | TOTALS |
|---|---|---|---|---|---|---|---|---|---|---|---|---|---|
| 1 Cash available | 5,000 | | | | | | | | | | | | 5,000 |
| INCOME | | | | | | | | | | | | | |
| Salary | 6,000 | 6,000 | 6,000 | 6,000 | 6,000 | 6,000 | 6,000 | 6,000 | 6,000 | 6,000 | 6,000 | 6,000 | 72,000 |
| 3 Self-employment net income | | | | | | | | | | | | | |
| 4 Investment income | | | | | | | | | | | | | |
| 5 TOTAL INCOME | 6,000 | 6,000 | 6,000 | 6,000 | 6,000 | 6,000 | 6,000 | 6,000 | 6,000 | 6,000 | 6,000 | 6,000 | 72,000 |
| 6 TOTAL CASH | 11,000 | 6,000 | 6,000 | 6,000 | 6,000 | 6,000 | 6,000 | 6,000 | 6,000 | 6,000 | 6,000 | 6,000 | 77,000 |
| EXPENSES | | | | | | | | | | | | | |
| 7 Taxes—personal property | 0 | 0 | 0 | 0 | 0 | 0 | 0 | 0 | 0 | 3,000 | 0 | 0 | 3,000 |
| 8 Taxes—real estate | 0 | 0 | 0 | 0 | 0 | 0 | 0 | 0 | 0 | 4,000 | 0 | 0 | 4,000 |
| 9 Home maintenance | 200 | 200 | 200 | 200 | 200 | 200 | 200 | 200 | 200 | 200 | 200 | 200 | 2,400 |
| 10 Food | 100 | 100 | 100 | 100 | 100 | 100 | 100 | 100 | 100 | 100 | 100 | 100 | 1,200 |
| 11 Household expenses | 500 | 500 | 500 | 500 | 500 | 500 | 500 | 500 | 500 | 500 | 500 | 500 | 6,200 |
| 12 Medical/dental | 150 | 50 | 230 | 150 | 50 | 50 | 150 | 50 | 50 | 150 | 50 | 50 | 1,200 |
| 13 Clothes | 700 | 500 | 500 | 500 | 500 | 1,500 | 500 | 500 | 1,500 | 500 | 500 | 500 | 8,200 |
| 14 Charitable contributions | 200 | 200 | 200 | 200 | 200 | 200 | 200 | 200 | 200 | MO | 200 | 200 | 2,400 |
| 15 Auto—gas/repairs | 200 | 200 | 200 | 200 | 200 | 200 | 200 | 200 | 200 | 200 | 200 | 200 | 2,400 |
| 16 Home mortgage | 1,400 | 1,400 | 1,400 | 1,400 | 1,400 | 1,400 | 1,400 | 1,400 | 1,400 | 1,400 | 1,400 | 1,400 | 16,800 |
| 17 Telephone—home | 100 | 100 | 100 | 100 | 100 | 100 | 100 | 100 | 100 | 100 | 100 | 100 | 1,200 |

(Continued)

# Sample Cash Flow Worksheet (continued)

| | SAMPLE | MAR | APR | MAY | JUN | JUL | AUG | SEP | OCT | NOV | DEC | JAN | FEB | TOTALS |
|---|---|---|---|---|---|---|---|---|---|---|---|---|---|---|
| 18 | Electric—home | 400 | 200 | 200 | 200 | 200 | 200 | 250 | 300 | 400 | 400 | 500 | 400 | 3,650 |
| 19 | Water—home | 65 | 65 | 150 | 150 | 150 | 100 | 100 | 100 | 65 | 65 | 65 | 65 | 1,140 |
| 20 | Cable—home | 48 | 48 | 48 | 48 | 48 | 48 | 48 | 48 | 48 | 48 | 48 | 48 | 576 |
| 21 | Business expense | 400 | 400 | 100 | 400 | 100 | 100 | 400 | 100 | 100 | 400 | 100 | 100 | 2,700 |
| 22 | Education | 0 | 0 | 0 | 0 | 0 | 0 | 0 | 0 | 0 | 0 | 0 | 0 | 0 |
| 23 | Insurance—life | 0 | 1,500 | 0 | 0 | 1,500 | 0 | 0 | 1,500 | 0 | 0 | 1,500 | 0 | 6,000 |
| 24 | Insurance—home | 0 | 0 | 0 | 0 | 0 | 0 | 0 | 0 | 0 | 0 | 0 | 0 | 0 |
| 25 | Insurance—car | 200 | 200 | 200 | 200 | 200 | 200 | 200 | 200 | 200 | 200 | 200 | 200 | 2,400 |
| 26 | Insurance—personal umbrella | 0 | 0 | 0 | 0 | 0 | 0 | 0 | 0 | 0 | 0 | 0 | 0 | 0 |
| 27 | Gifts | 50 | 50 | 50 | 50 | 50 | 50 | 50 | 50 | 50 | 50 | 50 | 50 | 600 |
| 28 | Vacations | 0 | 0 | 0 | 0 | 2,000 | 0 | 0 | 0 | 0 | 0 | 0 | 1,500 | 3,500 |
| 29 | Miscellaneous | 200 | 200 | 200 | 200 | 200 | 200 | 200 | 200 | 200 | 200 | 200 | 200 | 2,400 |
| 30 | Lessons | 245 | 245 | 245 | 0 | 0 | 0 | 245 | 245 | 245 | 245 | 245 | 245 | 2,205 |
| 31 | Camp | 0 | 1,000 | 0 | 0 | 0 | 0 | 0 | 0 | 0 | 0 | 0 | 0 | 1,000 |
| 32 | Bank loan #1 | 239 | 239 | 239 | 239 | 239 | 239 | 239 | 239 | 239 | 239 | 239 | 239 | 2,868 |
| 33 | Bank loan #2 | 300 | 300 | 300 | 300 | 300 | 300 | 300 | 300 | 300 | 300 | 300 | 300 | 3,600 |
| 34 | Bank loan #3 | 150 | 150 | 150 | 150 | 150 | 150 | 150 | 150 | 150 | 150 | 150 | 150 | 1,800 |
| 35 | Bank loan #4 | 200 | 200 | 200 | 200 | 200 | 200 | 200 | 200 | 200 | 200 | 200 | 200 | 2,400 |
| 36 | TOTAL EXPENSES | 6,047 | 8,047 | 5,532 | 5,487 | 8,587 | 6,037 | 5,732 | 6,882 | 6,447 | 12,847 | 7,047 | 6,947 | 85,839 |
| 37 | NET INCOME | 4,953 | (2,047) | 468 | 513 | (2,587) | (37) | 268 | (882) | (447) | (6847) | (1,047) | (947) | (8,639) |
| 38 | CUMULATIVE SURPLUS | 4,953 | 2,906 | 3,374 | 3,887 | 1,300 | 1,263 | 1,531 | 649 | 202 | (6,645) | (7,692) | (8,639) | |

Some expenses may be monthly; others are occasional. Periodic expenses may include car insurance, property and personal property taxes, safe deposit box fees, sanitation fees, some business expenses, and so on.

Monthly expenses usually include income and payroll taxes; household utilities, such as heating, electricity, and telephone; fixed real estate costs, such as condominium fees, rent, and mortgage; food, a category that includes general groceries; gasoline; credit card payments; and business expenses, such as wages, benefits, and office expenses.

The cash flow worksheet helps you plan around irregular income and expenses. Let's use life insurance costs as an example. Say the quarterly payment is due in April. In April's column, you write $1,500. For March and May, you write 0, because you don't pay anything then.

Your utility company can tell you how much you spent on heat and electricity for each month in the past year. If you prefer, most utility companies will put you on a plan that lets you pay the same amount every months for eleven months of the year, with any credits or debits made up in the last month.

You probably buy significant amounts of clothing twice a year: in August, before school and cold weather arrive, and just before and after the December holidays.

You probably celebrate the same gift-giving holidays every year. Instead of debating how much to spend when birthdays roll around, you can plan your gift expenditures now.

Vacations often happen in the summer, with a second season in the first quarter of the year, for those who go somewhere warm during the winter.

A smartphone app, such as Mint, Yogli, or iWallet, is a good way to keep track of the miscellaneous ways you spend your money. "Miscellaneous" will be your largest category at first. Work to minimize it. At the end, it should be your smallest category, because you will have discovered where your money goes and put expenditures into their proper buckets.

## Plan Your Future Cash Flow

Once you understand your past spending habits, you can plan your future cash flow. Begin your worksheet by filling in the current month. If you prefer, you can complete a full year's worksheet, from January to December. Remember, this is future cash flow, not a history of past spending.

For your first month, "total cash" is what you already have in the checking account, plus any other income that month. You may find that you have money left over at the end of the month, and it's very tempting to see that money and overspend.

Instead, use your cash flow statement to spot money that isn't working for you. If you see extra money sitting in your checking account every month, put it where it will earn more money. Figure 2.2 shows a surplus of $2,900 or more for March through June. As in this situation, if you have money in your account that you won't need for at least three months, put it in a certificate of deposit, a 13-week Treasury bill, or a money market mutual fund for that length of time and earn a higher rate of return.

## Plan Your Cash Reserve

How much money should you have in reserve? That depends on your cash flow. You need a fund that you can quickly tap in an emergency or to take advantage of a particularly good opportunity. Many financial advisors suggest having six months of household expenses in your reserve account. That number may or may not be right for you.

Your cash flow worksheet will help you determine how big your emergency/opportunity fund should be, by forecasting your likely expenditures. If you know that you'll need to pay your insurance premium in July, for instance, you'll be more likely to tuck aside surplus income in January.

Ultimately, the amount of your emergency fund is up to you. One of our clients keeps half a million dollars in his emergency fund. He doesn't need that much, but it makes him feel better. At the other extreme, some clients have no emergency fund and instead plan to tap a home equity line or business if they need extra money. It's a very personal decision. Look at your risks and your existing expenses, and pay attention to who you are and how much risk you're comfortable handling.

A cash flow worksheet can also indicate that you're spending more than you should. In this sample worksheet, we can see eight months that have negative cash flow, putting this person into a hole of $8,639 by year's end. Either income must increase or expenses must decrease when this is the case; you can't run your household on a deficit budget. You need to live on what you earn and have money left to invest for your future.

Now take out your accountant's paper or open up your spreadsheet. In the second column, list the months, beginning with the current month. In the first column, list your own income and expenses categories and fill in the numbers. Don't forget to include all the taxes you pay: federal and state income tax, plus other payroll taxes.

If you have a computer, consider using one of the excellent financial software programs, such as Quicken or Money. Software makes no arithmetic errors and is more sophisticated than paper spreadsheets. Not only will it handle cash flow and other worksheets, but software also lets you project what-if scenarios, automatically recalculating to show the consequences of any change.

## Income and Expenses Worksheets

The annual income and expenses worksheets in Figures 2.4 and 2.5 will jog your memory on all your income sources and all the ways you spend that money. For your own worksheets, enter the yearly amount for each sum that you will receive or spend in the coming year. You can use the data from the "totals" column of the cash flow worksheet to help you fill out the income and expenses worksheets. Check data from last year—look at tax forms and review your bank and credit card statements. Banks and credit card issuers will both send you new statements—all you need to do is ask. If you still don't know the exact amount for a particular item, make an estimate.

**FIGURE 2.4**

# Annual Income Worksheet

EARNED INCOME

    Salary                         _____

    Self-employment           _____

    Retirement                    _____

    Other earned income       _____

INVESTMENT INCOME

    Interest—taxable           _____

    Interest—federal and state exempt   _____

    Interest—federal tax exempt     _____

    Interest—state tax exempt       _____

    Interest—money market fund    _____

    Dividends                    _____

    Capital gains                _____

    Annuity                      _____

    Other                        _____

OTHER INCOME

    Social Security            _____

    Alimony received           _____

    Unemployment compensation   _____

    Other—not taxable         _____

    State and local income tax refund   _____

    Other—taxable              _____

BUSINESS INCOME

    Sales                        _____

    Gross receipts               _____

    Fees                         _____

    Other                        _____

FIGURE 2.4

# Annual Income Worksheet (continued)

UNCLASSIFIED INCOME

Now you see your cash flow and your annual income and expenses. Next, you'll calculate your tax bite.

## Spendable Cash Worksheet

The first step in doing this is to calculate your spendable cash. Figure 2.6 shows an example. You'll use the data from your other worksheets to fill in this form.

This worksheet shows you how your cash flow increases or decreases when you implement a particular financial strategy. If you buy more life insurance or increase your retirement contributions, for instance, how does your spendable cash change?

Notice that there are two columns to the right of each item description. The first column shows your present situation. The second one shows the effect of a hypothetical financial choice on that item. This sample shows the effect of putting money into an IRA: income taxes go down and spendable cash goes up by $860.

**FIGURE 2.5**

# Annual Expense Worksheet

INCOME & PAYROLL TAXES

    Federal Income Tax (FIT)—withheld      _____

    FIT—estimated payments      _____

    FIT—payment with return      _____

    State Income Tax (SIT)—withheld      _____

    SIT—estimated payment      _____

    SIT—payment with return      _____

    Local income tax      _____

    Social Security tax      _____

    State disability insurance      _____

    Income tax penalties      _____

HOUSEHOLD EXPENSES

    Fixed real estate      _____

    Maintenance and repairs      _____

    Real estate taxes      _____

    Home improvement      _____

    Furniture and decorating      _____

    Utilities      _____

    Personal property taxes      _____

    Vacation home expenses      _____

    Other      _____

PERSONAL EXPENSES

    Food      _____

    Personal allowances      _____

    Medical      _____

    Dental      _____

    Clothing and personal      _____

    Sales tax      _____

    Charitable contributions      _____

FIGURE 2.5

# Annual Expense Worksheet (continued)

Political contributions _____

Other _____

## TRANSPORTATION EXPENSES

Automobile _____

Other vehicles and equipment _____

Other transportation _____

## INVESTMENT/PROFESSIONAL EXPENSES

Investment management fees _____

Accounting fees _____

Legal fees—deductible _____

Legal fees—not deductible _____

Notary fees _____

Rental investment expense _____

Other _____

## INTEREST

Interest—home mortgage _____

Interest—consumer loans _____

Interest—credit cards _____

Penalty—early withdrawal _____

Bank service charge _____

## JOB RELATED EXPENSES

Unreimbursed business _____

Business education _____

Membership _____

Professional subscriptions _____

Moving _____

Child care _____

Other _____

*(Continued)*

**FIGURE 2.5**

# Annual Expense Worksheet (continued)

OTHER EXPENSES

    Education                      _____

    Alimony paid                 _____

    Child support                _____

    Casualty losses             _____

    Other                             _____

BUSINESS EXPENSES

    Cost of goods                _____

    Advertising                   _____

    Bad debts                     _____

    Bank service charges    _____

    Transportation              _____

    Commission                  _____

    Dues and publications   _____

    Employee wages            _____

    Employee benefits       _____

    Freight                         _____

    Insurance                     _____

    Interest                        _____

    Laundry and cleaning    _____

    Legal and professional  _____

    Office                           _____

    Pension and profit sharing  _____

    Rent                            _____

    Repairs                       _____

    Supplies and materials   _____

    Taxes                          _____

    Travel and entertainment  _____

    Utilities and telephone   _____

    Other                             _____

**FIGURE 2.6**

# Calculate Your Spendable Cash

|  | Scenario A | Scenario B |
|---|---|---|
| ADD INCOME: | | |
| 1. Business | _____ | _____ |
| 2. Salary or salaries | _____ | _____ |
| 3. Investment | _____ | _____ |
| 4. Other | _____ | _____ |
| 5. TOTAL INCOME | _____ | _____ |
| LESS: | | |
| 6. IRA | _____ | _____ |
| 7. Keogh | _____ | _____ |
| 8. Corporation retirement plans | _____ | _____ |
| 9. 401(k) | _____ | _____ |
| 10. Public employee retirement system | _____ | _____ |
| 11. State teacher retirement system | _____ | _____ |
| 12. 403(b) tax-deferred annuity | _____ | _____ |
| 13. Medical/dental plans | _____ | _____ |
| 14. Disability plans | _____ | _____ |
| 15. Business expenses | _____ | _____ |
| 16. Depreciation | _____ | _____ |
| 17. Normal deductions | _____ | _____ |
| 18. Exemptions | _____ | _____ |
| 19. TAXABLE INCOME | _____ | _____ |
| LESS: | | |
| 20. Taxes (for illustration only) | _____ | _____ |
| ADD BACK FROM ABOVE: | | |
| 21. Depreciation | _____ | _____ |
| 22. Exemptions | _____ | _____ |
| 23. Nontaxable income | _____ | _____ |
| LESS: | | |
| 24. Retirement savings | _____ | _____ |
| 25. Medical/dental expenses | _____ | _____ |
| 26. Disability insurance | _____ | _____ |
| 27. Life insurance | _____ | _____ |
| 28. Education | _____ | _____ |
| 29. Certain living expenses | _____ | _____ |
| 30. SPENDABLE CASH | _____ | _____ |
| 31. CASH FLOW INCREASE | _____ | |

© 1988 by John E. Sestina.

As you fill out this worksheet, note that it first takes out depreciation, exemptions, and nontaxable income (lines 21, 22, and 23) and then adds them back in. These items are tax deductible but don't involve any cash outlay. An accountant, tax preparer, or financial planner can estimate your depreciation for you using IRS Form 4562. Exemptions are shown on IRS Schedule 1040.

Figure 2.7 shows your spendable cash worksheet.

---

**FIGURE 2.7**

# Spendable Cash Worksheet

|                                           | Current  | Proposed |
|-------------------------------------------|----------|----------|
| ADD INCOME:                               |          |          |
| 1. Business                               |          |          |
| 2. Salary or salaries                     | $41,360  | $41,360  |
| 3. Investment                             |          |          |
| 4. Other                                  |          |          |
| 5. TOTAL INCOME                           | 41,360   | 41,360   |
| LESS:                                     |          |          |
| 6. IRA                                    |          | 4,000    |
| 7. Keogh                                  |          |          |
| 8. Corporation retirement plans           |          |          |
| 9. 401(k)                                 |          |          |
| 10. Public employee retirement system     |          |          |
| 11. State teacher retirement system       |          |          |
| 12. 403(b) tax-deferred annuity           |          |          |
| 13. Medical/dental plans                  |          |          |
| 14. Disability plans                      |          |          |
| 15. Business expenses                     |          |          |
| 16. Depreciation (Form 4562)              |          |          |
| 17. Normal deductions                     | 3,760    | 3,760    |

## FIGURE 2.7

# Spendable Cash Worksheet (continued)

| | Current | Proposed |
|---|---|---|
| 18. Exemptions (Schedule 1040) | 7,600 | 7,600 |
| 19. TAXABLE INCOME | 30,000 | 26,000 |
| LESS: | | |
| 20. Income taxes (for illustration only) | 4,640 | 3,780 |
| ADD BACK FROM ABOVE: | | |
| 21. Depreciation (Form 4562) | | |
| 22. Exemptions (Schedule 1040) | 7,600 | 7,600 |
| 23. Nontaxable income | | |
| LESS: | | |
| 24. Retirement savings | 4,000 | IRA |
| 25. Medical/dental expenses | | |
| 26. Disability insurance | | |
| 27. Life insurance | | |
| 28. Education | | |
| 29. Certain living expenses | | |
| 30. SPENDABLE CASH | $28,960 | $29,820 |
| 31. CASH FLOW INCREASE | $860 | |

## Balance Sheet: What Is Your Financial Worth?

You're almost done with these baseline worksheets! It's time to fill out a balance sheet. Figure 2.8 shows an example. By now, you may be seeing numbers in your sleep. Stick with it. The fun part is about to begin.

A balance sheet is a snapshot of your financial status taken once a year (or more often, if a year brings major changes). It tells you how you're doing in your quest to achieve your goals and lets you see progress or regression when you compare last year's balance sheet against this year's

**FIGURE 2.8**

# Balance Sheet

**ASSETS**                                    **Date:** _____

CURRENT ASSETS

    Cash on hand                          _____

    Checking accounts                     _____

    Money market accounts                 _____

    Savings accounts                      _____

    Treasury bills                        _____

    Life insurance cash value             _____

    Escrow account                        _____

    Other current assets                  _____

TOTAL CURRENT ASSETS                                      _____

MARKETABLE INVESTMENTS

    Common stocks                         _____

    Preferred stocks                      _____

    Treasury bonds                        _____

    Corporate bonds                       _____

    Municipal bonds                       _____

    Unit investment trust                 _____

    REIT (Real Estate Investment Trust) shares   _____

    Mutual funds                          _____

    Traded stock options                  _____

    Warrants                              _____

    Futures contracts                     _____

    Other marketable investments          _____

TOTAL MARKETABLE INVESTMENTS                              _____

LONG-TERM INVESTMENTS

    Real estate                           _____

    Farming interests                     _____

    Oil and gas investments               _____

# Balance Sheet (continued)

| | |
|---|---|
| Tax shelters | _____ |
| Leasing investments | _____ |
| Research & development ventures | _____ |
| Venture capital investment | _____ |
| Annuities | _____ |
| Deposits | _____ |
| Long-term receivables | _____ |
| Mortgage receivables | _____ |
| Interest-free loan receivables | _____ |
| Stock purchase plan | _____ |
| Executive stock options | _____ |
| Investment collections | _____ |
| Precious metals | _____ |
| Mineral royalties | _____ |
| Closely held businesses | _____ |
| Other long-term assets | _____ |
| **TOTAL LONG-TERM ASSETS** | _____ |
| | |
| RETIREMENT/DEFERRED ASSETS | |
| IRA | _____ |
| Keogh account | _____ |
| Retirement plan | _____ |
| Deferred compensation plan | _____ |
| Other retirement plans | _____ |
| **TOTAL RETIREMENT/DEFERRED ASSETS** | _____ |
| | |
| TRUST AND ESTATE ASSETS | |
| Trust assets | _____ |
| Estate assets | _____ |
| **TOTAL TRUST AND ESTATE ASSETS** | _____ |

*(Continued)*

**FIGURE 2.8**

# Balance Sheet (continued)

PERSONAL/NONEARNING ASSETS

    Residence            _____

    Vacation property       _____

    Automobiles          _____

    Home furnishings      _____

    Other personal property   _____

    Noninvestment collection  _____

    Other vehicles and equipment  _____

    Other nonearning assets   _____

TOTAL PERSONAL/NONEARNING ASSETS         _____

BUSINESS ASSETS

    Cash account         _____

    Checking account      _____

    Accounts receivable    _____

    Short-term investments   _____

    Deposits            _____

    Inventory           _____

    Land               _____

    Buildings           _____

    Furniture and fixtures    _____

    Manufacturing equipment  _____

    Transportation equipment  _____

    Office equipment      _____

    Other fixed assets     _____

    Other assets         _____

TOTAL BUSINESS ASSETS          _____

---

**FIGURE 2.8**

# Balance Sheet (continued)

UNCLASSIFIED ASSETS

  Unclassified assets         _____

TOTAL UNCLASSIFIED ASSETS                 _____

TOTAL ASSETS                                 _____

**LIABILITIES**

CURRENT LIABILITIES

  Credit cards         _____

  Demand notes         _____

  Margin accounts         _____

  Other         _____

TOTAL CURRENT LIABILITIES             _____

LONG-TERM LIABILITIES

  Home mortgage         _____

  Home improvement loan         _____

  Other real estate mortgages         _____

  Automobile loans         _____

  Student loan         _____

  Loan on life insurance         _____

  Investment liabilities         _____

  Interest-free loan payable         _____

  Other long-term liabilities         _____

TOTAL LONG-TERM LIABILITIES             _____

BUSINESS LIABILITIES

  Accounts payable         _____

  Accrued expenses         _____

  Prepaid orders         _____

  Employment taxes         _____

*(Continued)*

**FIGURE 2.8**

# Balance Sheet (continued)

BUSINESS LIABILITIES (*continued*)

Accredited FICA tax _____

Other payroll taxes _____

Long-term loans _____

Other liabilities _____

TOTAL BUSINESS LIABILITIES _____

UNCLASSIFIED LIABILITIES

Unclassified liabilities _____

TOTAL UNCLASSIFIED LIABILITIES _____

TOTAL LIABILITIES _____

NET WORTH (TOTAL ASSETS – TOTAL LIABILITIES) _____

model. Ideally, of course, it will show a net worth that grows as you work toward your target.

## Evaluate Your Data

By now, you have an impressive stack of wish lists and worksheets. You may also feel like you're ready to sit for the Certified Public Accountant (CPA) exam. Rest easy. The worst of the intense calculations is over.

Now comes the moment of truth: comparing your dreams to your financial facts. Look at each item on your wish list. How close or how far are you from achieving that goal? How much more do you need? Is one goal a higher priority than another? You might prefer a new car over a vacation or feel that sending your children to college is better than leaving them a big estate.

Get some more blank paper (a notebook is handy) and write down priorities, recommendations, and alternatives as you read through the rest of the book.

## Develop Recommendations and Alternate Solutions

So how do you get from here to wherever you want to go? That's what the rest of this book is about: helping you lower those taxes, increase your investments, improve your cash flow, and reduce estate taxes.

## Summary

Locate all your financial data, set up a storage system, and keep the information available. Use the checklists and forms to show you where you are and where you want to be. Complete all the forms:

- Cash flow worksheet
- Income and expenses worksheet
- Tax calculation worksheet
- Spendable cash worksheet
- Balance sheet

Include your spouse and financial advisors in these processes. They are important participants and can bring different perspectives to your plan.

# CHAPTER 3

# Retirement

## Planning for Financial Independence

This book's most important goal is to help you achieve financial independence. When you can manage to be wealthy, then retirement doesn't have to mean rocking chairs and pinching pennies. It can mean financial independence.

In the Introduction, you learned the real reason why people invest: because someday they'll no longer be able to work. When you achieve financial freedom, it doesn't matter if the boss fires you. If you want to work at your current job or a more appealing one, you can. If you don't want to work, you don't have to. Remember, as you work through the calculations in this chapter, your goal is financial independence. The choice of whether and when to retire will be up to you.

Now it's time to learn the true cost of financial freedom. Hide the keys to the liquor cabinet, abandon the ice cream and candy stores, and let's begin. Estimating how much money you will need for retirement and how much you'll need to save each year to meet that goal may be a shock. It's better to find out what it takes now, rather than later. The sooner you start saving, the less you have to save each year, because you'll have more time to save and your money will have more time to grow. We'll discuss more about how to get the most from your savings in Chapter 9.

In this chapter, I'll review the information you need to gather and you'll learn how to calculate:

1. How much you need for retirement living expenses.

2. How much your current retirement savings will be worth when you retire.

**3.** How much you still need to save each year in order to accumulate a lump sum that will earn an annual sum equal to the amount in item 1 by the time you retire.

Maybe you think you can't save as much as you'll need. In this chapter, you'll see how strategies such as deferring taxes on your savings interest can greatly reduce the amount you must save each year and still meet your goal.

## Review Your Retirement Goals

Before you can plan for your retirement, you need to know what you want. If you only read through the first two chapters and didn't put your thoughts down on paper, please go back and do it now. Chapter 1 has specific questions that must be answered before you can move through this chapter.

Do you hope to quit your existing job to start a business in which you've always been interested? Expand an existing second business? Volunteer for a cause? Pursue personal passions or spend more time with family? Whatever you choose, a plan for financial independence puts you in control.

As you plan for retirement, be honest with yourself about the different possible outcomes over the next decade or more ahead of you. Consider at least one scenario in which your health substantially changes. How would this change your plan? Work with your planner to develop a spendable cash worksheet showing how your finances would change.

## Your Cash Flow Worksheet Is Crucial

If you have not already done your cash flow worksheet, please stop reading and go back to Chapter 2. You need those numbers. How can you estimate what you'll need in retirement if you don't know how much you live on today? I know you will be tempted to skip all that hard work and just estimate that you make $50,000 a year now, so that's what you need to live on in retirement. Don't make that mistake! Completing the cash flow worksheet takes time, but this is your life and your money we're talking about. Who cares more about them than you do? This information is the foundation of your present and your future. Take the time to make it solid.

Many people think they know what they spend each year. They have absolutely no idea. You may spend less than your income, but the sad fact is that many people spend more than they earn. Until you do a cash flow worksheet, you will not know the truth. That's what this book is all about: finally finding out the truth about your finances, setting goals, planning how to reach them, and putting your plan into action. Bite the bullet and go back to Chapter 2. I'll wait for you.

After you've finished your cash flow worksheet, look again at your retirement goals. You may want to revise them now or wait until you've completed the following calculations. Review your goals with your family.

## Assumptions for Retirement Planning

Before you calculate how much you should save for retirement, you must understand the assumptions on which your plan will be built.

1.  These calculations do not include Social Security. I believe you need to rely on yourself, not on the government, to take care of you. I'm not debating the need for this program or its future, merely saying that being prepared to provide all your retirement funds will give you peace of mind and control over your future.

2.  Use conservative numbers. It's better to overestimate your needs than to underestimate them. Use inflation numbers, rates of return, or other variable numbers that make you comfortable, not necessarily those in the examples. This is your future and your money.

3.  Remember the cardinal rule: you will not touch your retirement fund principal. You will live off the interest, ensuring that you won't run out of money, no matter how long you live. There are retirement savings calculations that include living off the principal and interest, eventually reducing your fund to zero. Those calculations

are beyond the scope of this book and require input from specialized professionals.

4. To show you how to estimate your retirement fund, I use one inflation rate, one investment rate of return, and one tax rate, assuming that these rates will stay the same during all the years from now through the end of your life. In real life, that's not very likely, but the numbers we have now are better than no numbers at all.

The following example is meant as a guide to show how much you may need to save for retirement. Work through this calculation to understand the factors that help determine how much you'll need for retirement. For your own situation, choose conservative rate assumptions, aiming for an estimate that will be more than you need, not less. For exact calculations, online calculators such as Kiplinger's and/or conversations with a financial planner can help you perform exact calculations.

## Answer These Questions before Doing the Calculations

First, find out how much it costs for you to live today: the information on your cash flow worksheet. Using that worksheet and your wish list, consider what may be different when you retire. Take another sheet of accounting paper (or start a new computer spreadsheet page) estimate your cash flow during retirement.

## Estimating Retirement Cash Flow

Use the following questions to help you adjust the numbers. Don't worry about the effects of inflation now. I'll show you how to allow for that later. For now, look at each item and estimate the changes in your cash flow worksheet when you retire. Ask yourself:

1. Will the house be paid off, or will you move to a smaller house with lower monthly payments?

2. Will you have a fixed or variable rate mortgage, or will you pay rent?

3. How many people must you support? You may have a houseful of children now, but you will have only you (and your spouse, if you're married) when you retire.

4. Will you do less traveling or more?

5. Will you spend less or more on clothing, cars, meals, and miscellaneous items?

6. What other costs will increase or decrease, such as healthcare expenses?

Of course, there is a variable you cannot predict: your health. Most people over 60 years old remain in good health for many years, though of course older people can expect to use more healthcare than younger people, all other things being equal. If you know that your health costs will increase because of family history or other factors, then you may want to increase those costs for this estimate. Make the changes that seem right for you.

In our example, we'll assume living expenses of $18,000 per year in today's pretax dollars.

## Other Factors That Will Affect Your Retirement Needs

You've got a sense of how much money you'll need in retirement. There are a few other questions you must also answer in order to calculate your retirement needs.

1. How old are you now?

2. At what age would you like to retire?

3. How many years do you have until retirement?

4. How long will you live? Go to www.ssa.gov/oact/population/longevity.html and adjust the answer as you see fit, given your own health and family history. I include this question to make you think about how many years of retirement you will have. As I said earlier, these calculations are based on the assumption that you will live on your investment interest—not principal. By leaving the principal

untouched, you'll always have money to live on, no matter how long you live.

5.  In the past 30 years, the average annual increase in inflation has been about 6 percent. You may want to use a higher or lower figure. Pick a number that makes you comfortable. Over the past 70 years, inflation has averaged 3 percent. I use the 6 percent suggested by the shorter time frame. If I am wrong, the client has more money.

It's possible to do these retirement calculations using a varying inflation rate, but those calculations are beyond the scope of this book. A computer program and/or a qualified fee-only financial planner can help you in doing this more complex calculation if you feel it is necessary.

6.  What rate of return will your investments earn? Again, you must pick one rate in order to do these calculations. Ask a qualified financial planner to help you if you want to vary the rates of return over time. Pick a conservative rate. If your money earns more, it will be a pleasant surprise.

## Don't Forget about Taxes

What is your tax rate? Refer to Chapter 2 for a simple way to calculate your taxes. If you didn't originally include federal, state, and local taxes in your cash flow worksheet, go back now and include taxes. You must know all your living expenses, including all your taxes, before you can do the rest of the calculations. You may want to increase or decrease the tax rate, depending on your circumstances.

Lacking a crystal ball, your only good choice is to pick the highest tax rate you think you might pay. According to the U.S. Department of Commerce, the maximum effective tax rate levied to date was 94 percent during World War II. The current top rate is 39.6 percent. Who knows what it might be when you retire? For this calculation, it's better to pick a rate that is too high and end up with more money than to underestimate and scramble to pay your bills. For this example, I'll choose 30 percent as our highest expected tax rate.

## How Much Money Will You Need?

With answers to those questions in hand, you can calculate how much money you will need for the first year of retirement; www.mutualofomaha.com/tools/calculators/retirement-planning/how-does-inflation-impact-my-retirement-income-needs.php can help you do this.

## What Lump Sum Will Yield the Money You Need?

Next, find out how much you must have in a lump sum to live off the interest only; www.mutualofomaha.com/tools/calculators/retirement-planning/are-my-current-retirement-savings-sufficient.php can help you make this calculation.

Or, if you prefer, take the gross annual retirement cost in inflated dollars and divide it by the gross rate of return.

Using the numbers from our example: $147,598 divided by 0.07 equals $2,108,543.

To earn $147,598 in interest each year at a 7 percent gross rate of return, you'll need to invest slightly more than $2.1 million.

That sounds like a lot of money, doesn't it? It certainly would be now. We all tend to forget the effects of inflation. Remember the 20-cent postage stamp? That was in 1981. In 1971, a stamp cost 8 cents. If you're over 40, do you remember when ground beef cost 39 cents a pound? That was in 1962.

For the most part, inflated prices creep up on us. Believe the calculations. If you want to live on $18,000 in today's dollars and all the other numbers are the same as those in our example, then you need to have more than $2.1 million invested for the first year of your retirement. The after-tax yield will give you the equivalent of $18,000 each year.

## How Much Do You Have in Savings?

You know how much you need. How are you going to get that money? First, look at how much you've already saved. Go back to the balance sheet you created in Chapter 2. Your retirement savings should be listed there under Assets/Retirement/Deferred Investments. You also may want to include other investments: marketable, long term, and so on. Whatever you currently have set aside for retirement in a lump sum, find those numbers in your balance sheet and total them. Don't include future contributions. If you haven't already completed your balance sheet, do it now. Start with solid data, or your final estimate will be unreliable.

If your pension or profit-sharing plan will calculate an annual benefit for you, subtract that yearly amount from the annual inflated dollar amount that you calculated you would need. Or if they tell you what your lump-sum benefit will be worth when you retire, subtract that from the total retirement fund you'll need.

A cautionary note: if your company tells you how much your future benefit will be, ask what that benefit includes. Some companies include Social Security as part of the benefit total. Find out just what the company will pay you. If you happen to also qualify for Social Security, then you'll have that much extra.

If you don't know your projected benefit, you can calculate it. For this part of our example, let's assume that your current retirement savings are in a taxable investment. We will discuss the advantages of tax deferral for your retirement savings later in this chapter.

## Gross versus Net Investment Rate

Whenever you determine the value of your savings, you must consider taxes. If the interest is taxable, then you must calculate your actual net rate, after taxes are taken out. Take the gross investment rate of return and multiply it by your total tax rate. Include federal, state, and local taxes. The result is the percent lost to taxes. Subtract that from your gross rate to get the net rate.

To simplify the calculations, let's round up the net rate of return to 5 percent.

## Future Value of Current Retirement Savings

Now calculate what your current retirement savings will be worth when you need it. Let's say you have $10,000, the gross rate of return is 7 percent, the net rate is 5 percent, and you earn interest for 30 years.

This next point is crucial: you must leave it alone. Don't touch the principal or the interest. Let it accumulate. Don't buy a new car with it. Don't take a trip with it. Don't buy new clothes with it. That money is not available. If you leave it alone, then today's $10,000 will grow at the after-tax rate of 5 percent to $43,200 in 30 years.

But if you spend the interest you earn every year, in 30 years you will have exactly the same amount of money you have now: $10,000. See how important it is to leave the principal and interest alone?

Your $10,000 today increases to $43,200 in 30 years. Now take the total retirement fund needed, $2,108,543, and subtract $43,200. You still need $2,065,343 to retire.

## How Much Do You Still Need to Save Each Year?

Where will you get that $2 million? It comes from your savings, which you then invest. Next you'll learn how to calculate how much you need to save each year to accumulate that $2 million. You must know how much you need before you can decide how to invest. You'll get to the fun part, reducing taxes and investing, in a little while.

You know you need $2 million. You know you have 30 years in which to save at a rate of 5 percent. Go to www.bloomberg.com/personal-finance/calculators/retirement and type in these values.

There it is in stark black and white. Each year for the next 30 years, the person in our example will need to save **$30,435.86** and must earn about $45,000 before taxes—in addition to the money it takes to live today—to put that amount in savings.

Do your own calculation to see your own needs.

## What If You Can't Save That Much?

Don't let these numbers fluster you; this is not a cut-and-dried process. Go back and look at all the assumptions you made in reaching this final number. Maybe you were pessimistic and put inflation at 10 percent. Reducing that number (only if you are comfortable doing so) will reduce the final amount you need. There's nothing anyone can do to change the historical inflation numbers. However, there are things you can do to lower your savings goal and still retire. Here are your four alternatives:

**1.** Earn more money

**2.** Reduce your taxes

**3.** Increase your rate of return

**4.** Change your goals

## Can You Earn More Money?

The most obvious solution is to make more money. Assess your skills. Should you be earning more at your present job or seeking a better-paying one? If you are already working a number of jobs, you're at your limit. If you have only one job, can you take a second job? Better yet, can you start your own sideline business? I'll discuss starting a business in more detail later, and you'll see why they have so many advantages for increasing income and reducing taxes.

## Can You Reduce Your Taxes?

If you've been earning money, paying taxes, and then trying to save, there's a better way: save pretax dollars through an IRA, a 401(k), or a pension plan. By deferring taxes, you have more left over to spend now, and you increase your rate of return. As a result, you'll need less money in your total fund, so you don't have to save as much now.

If we save money in a tax-deferred account in our example, our $10,000 would grow to $76,100, instead of only $43,200. You would only have to save about $22,000 per year, instead of almost $45,000. That's quite an incentive to learn about tax deferral!

There are other ways to reduce your taxes legally, which I'll talk about in Chapter 8.

## Can You Increase Your Rate of Return?

In addition to decreasing the tax bite, can you increase the rate of return on your investments? If you've been earning 2 percent in a savings account, can you earn 3 percent by putting your savings in a long-term certificate of deposit? If you've been earning 3 percent in a CD, can you earn 5 percent in a different investment? Increasing your rate of return means you have less to put in savings.

By increasing your gross rate of return from 7 percent to 9 percent per year and deferring taxes, you'll need a smaller total lump sum. Our example's $10,000 would grow to $132,700, and you would need to save only about $11,000 per year, or about one-fourth of the amount needed in the original calculation, where interest was taxable and the return on investment was lower. See how good financial planning can help you manage to be wealthy?

Of course, you will have to determine what level of investment risk is comfortable for you. Usually, the higher the long-term rate of return, the greater the investment's short-term risk. If increasing your long-term rate of return from 7 percent to 9 percent means you lose sleep because the investment has more short-term risk, don't do it.

However, most people can increase their rate of return without greatly increasing their risk, just by having a financial plan. You'll learn the details in Chapter 9.

## Can You Change Your Goal?

Finally, can you change your goal? As you read Chapter 1, you wrote down your dreams. I believe that most of us can achieve our goals if we commit to reaching them. Remember, too, that you still have more strategies to learn about. The rest of this book will cover all the information you need to know about reducing taxes, improving your investment savvy, and meeting your goals.

For now, take another hard look at your other goals. What are your priorities? If you can fund only one goal, which one should it be? Maybe you can fund part of two goals. The decisions are up to you.

This is why personal financial planning is so important. Don't be fooled into thinking some computer printout will be right for you. You need to do your own calculations.

Here are three ways you might change your goal.

**1.** Retire later. Maybe your goal is to retire at age 55. If you wait until age 60, you will need to save less per year now.

**2.** Live on less per year. Perhaps your estimate included traveling six months a year. If you reduce that to three months, you'll need less money every year. Maybe your list contains other luxuries. Can you reduce them?

**3.** Retire from one job and start or expand a second business. Or perhaps you could retire from one job and, rather than earning no income, start working part time at another job. That plan would reduce the amount you need to save.

Now you understand the importance of doing all the homework in Chapters 1 and 2. Decide what (if any) assumptions about your retirement or your current lifestyle to change.

## But What About ...?

I know some of you have some questions.

**1.** What about inflation during retirement?

**2.** Why can't I just live off the principal and interest when I retire? Then I won't have to save as much now.

**3.** What if my health fails?

### Inflation and Retirement

What about inflation after you retire? That's a good question. Most of us remember the double-digit inflation of 1974 and 1979 to 1981. Unfortunately, no one has a crystal ball that can predict inflation.

We can only look at past trends. Historically, inflation has averaged about 6 percent a year over the past 30 years.

The previous calculations assume that inflation will be a level number. History tells us that this is unlikely—inflation rates will probably vary over the coming years. I've used a constant rate for two reasons. First, it makes the calculations simpler to do and understand.

Second, inflation will probably be less of a problem for you after you retire. When you retire, you tend to slip out of inflation's mainstream. We notice inflation when we buy things: housing, clothing, travel, and so forth. Retirees often spend less than working people. Depending on their health, of course, they may spend the first four or five years traveling. Then they cut back on travel. They don't need work wardrobes. They likely own their homes, and they keep that house in good shape by taking the time to maintain it. They may not need new cars as often as they did when they were working, because they don't drive to an office every day.

Remember that every year, you're dealt a new deck of cards for inflation and taxes. The issue is not this year's rate, whether or not you reach your goal.

## Using Up Your Retirement Fund

As previously discussed, these calculations figure the amount of money you need in order to live on the interest, without touching principal. If you plan to live on principal as well as interest, you will need to save less money.

There is one major problem with this approach: you have to know how long you're going to live. If you live longer than that, you'll be out of money!

Look again at www.ssa.gov/oact/population/longevity.html, and at your family to see the age of the longest-living person of your gender. Live longer than that person, and you'll be broke. Yes, you could buy a lifetime annuity, but you'll probably do better by investing on your own.

Go to www.calculator.net/annuity-payout-calculator.html to see the numbers. For peace of mind, however, living off your investments' interest is the gold standard.

## Health Concerns

Because much news is bad news, we read or hear more about retired people with health problems. According to experts, most people over 60 are actually in good health. The problems of health planning for the retired are beyond the scope of this book.

There are entire courses devoted to health planning for the retired and are available from your local senior center, social service agency, or AARP (formerly the American Association of Retired Persons).

Remember that a health savings account, or HSA, can be a source of healthcare funding when you are in retirement. If you have a high-deductible healthcare plan now, you can contribute more money than you currently need to your HSA, invest the excess, and use it to pay your Medicare premiums, drug plan premiums, and out-of-pocket medical costs after you stop working.

Now you know how much money you need to save each year to fund your retirement goal. As you read the following chapters, make notes about which tools and strategies will help you better meet that goal. As you learn how to manage to be wealthy, you will be able to meet your goal sooner, increase your goal, or reduce your per-year savings requirements for that goal.

## Summary

**1.** Review your retirement goals from Chapter 1.

**2.** Create your projected retirement cash flow worksheet.

**3.** Choose an inflation rate, investment rate of return, and so on according to your comfort level. Check your balance sheet to see how much you have already saved. Then calculate the future worth of those dollars. Calculate how much you will need to save each year. If it will be difficult or impossible to reach your goal, consider these four alternatives:

**1.** Earn more money

**2.** Reduce your taxes

**3.** Increase your rate of return

**4.** Change your goal

By using one or more of these strategies, you can meet your goal of financial independence.

# CHAPTER 4

# Planning to Send Your Children to College

In this chapter, I'll show you how to calculate the cost of giving your children a college education. You'll also learn various ways to provide that education at the lowest possible cost. No matter what methods you choose, share your thinking and planning with your child.

## How Much Will a College Degree Cost?

Both public and private college costs have increased at a higher rate than inflation since 1986. Pretty sobering, isn't it? The following step-by-step plan will help you analyze your needs and fulfill your goal of sending your children to college.

Go back to the educational goals you wrote down in Chapter 1. In this chapter, you'll fill in the details, determining how much it will cost to meet your goals.

First, you must answer these questions:

1. How many children will go to college?
2. What are their current ages?
3. How many years until each one enters college?
4. How many years will they attend school?
5. What is the current cost (tuition, fees, room, and board) of the college they will attend? You can get this from a college's website, or you can call the college and ask. You may not yet know where your

child will attend college. If that's the case, you can still get a sense of current prices. Investigate the cost of attending a top private school, a top public school, and a public university in your state. *U.S. News and World Report*'s annual college rankings are a good source of information about which schools are considered the best in their categories.

**6.** Choose an annual inflation rate. I can't tell you what specific number to use, because I can't accurately predict how much faster than overall inflation college costs will rise. You may feel that 12 percent is right, or you may choose a higher or lower number based on your beliefs about inflation and other factors.

Do any of your children have special needs? Whether they have asthma or a learning disability, you already know what additional resources you have needed up to this point. If your child is younger or has just recently had a special needs diagnosis, contact your support group or special needs professional consultant, as well as your financial planner, to estimate what additional costs to factor into your plan.

The calculators at the site www.savingforcollege.com, particularly www.savingforcollege.com/college-savings-calculator, can help you project how much college will cost and how much you should begin saving now in order to meet that expense.

## Where Will You Find the Money?

You have several choices in funding your children's education. The worst method is to wait until the child is accepted to a college or university and then try to come up with the money. I've seen people bankrupt themselves trying to put their kids through college.

A second method is to put money aside each year, starting now, until your children are finished with school. This is the method that most of you should probably use, and I'll talk more about how to do that later.

The third way involves setting aside a lump sum now and investing it, with the goal of growing it to the same size as the cost of sending them to school. This is the least expensive method and the best, if you can manage it.

Let's look at what each of the three methods will cost.

## Pay as You Go

We estimate it will cost a total of $90,344 to put the two children in our example through college. Plug in your own figures to estimate your education dollar needs.

## Save Each Year

If the family in the example decided to start saving today, how much would they need to save each year? We figured the future cost. Let's assume that they invest the money to earn 8 percent every year, and that they let all the principal and interest compound. An online calculator can help us do this. Go to www.savingforcollege.com/college-savings-calculator/index.php?childs_age=12&page=results. Fill in the information the page requests.

To have the necessary funds in hand at the time the first child starts college, this family needs to begin saving and investing $1,146 every month.

## Invest a Lump Sum Early

In the third method, a family puts aside a lump sum now and lets the interest compound until the children start college. Every year, the parents withdraw only the amount necessary to fund that year of school. This method requires the least parental investment.

Using the lump sum method, our imaginary family would need to invest just $40,000 today at 8 percent interest. In eight years, they will have the estimated $90,000 they'll needed to fund two college educations.

Notice the difference in total costs. Remember, whichever method you choose, the numbers we show here are the net amount, without considering taxes. Fortunately, there are tax-advantaged ways to save for education expenses, which we will discuss shortly.

## Review Your Goals

Now you know the facts. Look at your original educational goals. You may need to revise them.

If it isn't possible to meet your educational goals, what can you do?

There are always five alternatives when it looks as if a goal is not reachable:

1. Increase your income

2. Reduce your taxes

3. Reduce your spending

4. Change your goal

5. Take more risk with your investments

There it is in black and white, no more and no less. You must choose one or more alternatives from this short list. As you will see in later chapters, there are dozens of ways to put these alternatives into action.

For the rest of this chapter, we'll focus on specific ways to meet your education goal. The first rule in meeting any financial goal is this: the sooner you save, the better. You've seen its power from earlier calculations, so let compound interest work for you. It's not too soon to start saving for college when your child is born—or even before.

Do you want or need to fund all of your children's educations? Consider expecting your children to earn part of their educational funds. It can encourage a work ethic, make them partly responsible for whether they can have the benefits of a college education, and increase their commitment to make the most of their college years. Discuss this goal with your planner so they understand that you don't expect to fully fund your children's education. Your planner can evaluate whether some of the strategies mentioned in this chapter, such as splitting, are appropriate for you.

If your children are in high school now, what are the possibilities for scholarships and other financial aid? Many college websites offer financial aid calculators that can give you a rough idea of how much need-based aid your child might receive from that institution. In some instances private schools can offer a net price that is less than the cost of attending a public school, because private schools typically have greater financial resources and flexibility than their public counterparts.

Merit-based and sports scholarships are other options, as are scholarships from your employer, fraternal, or sororal organizations, professional organizations, or other groups. There are scholarships available based on national ancestry, future professional plans—would your child like to be a veterinarian who works on cows in Tennessee?—and essay competitions. Many of them offer small awards, but the money can add up.

Family members, particularly grandparents, may be willing to help. Grandparents who directly fund a grandchild's education pay no gift tax on the money, even though the funds leave their estate, so long as they write a check directly to the school.

Parents who work at a college or university may be able to take courses or have family members take courses at reduced or no cost. Some schools have reciprocal arrangements that allow the children of their employees to attend another school at a discounted rate.

Different states provide differing amounts of state aid. For example, California state schools are free to California residents. In every case, public schools are less expensive for in-state residents than for their out-of-state peers.

## Who Controls the Money?

Will you control the education fund, or will it be in your children's names? Everyone has different feelings about this issue, and it's vital that you consider it.

We all hope that our children will grow up to be a credit to us and make a contribution to society. But let's face it: despite all possible good parenting efforts, some kids don't turn out as well as their parents hoped. If education funds are in their names, they may use that money to buy a car instead of a year of school.

If your children decide not to go to college, would you give them whatever amount of money you've saved anyway? If they control the money, then the money is theirs. If you control the money and they announce that they're dropping out of school, but still want the money, then you can decide whether to give them all, some, or none of it. Control gives you more flexibility.

# Effects of Tax Laws on Your Education Goal

We'll discuss understanding and working with the complicated changes of recent tax laws in detail in the tax chapter. What follows here is a brief summary. These changes will significantly affect your educational planning.

## Taxing Scholarships

Extra scholarship money—funds that equal more than the combined cost of tuition, fees, and books—are taxed at the child's rate. This includes special scholarships for athletic, musical, or other skills. In a sense, this is a good problem to have, in that it means that college costs are covered. Your child may even be able to attend a more expensive school, if that's appropriate.

## Student Loans

The interest paid on student loans is tax deductible. If your student qualifies, federally backed student loans offer better rates and more flexible repayment terms than do private loans. You should not borrow money yourself to fund your child's education. Your child can get a loan, if that's an appropriate solution. No one will loan you the money you need for retirement.

## Education IRA/Coverdell Account, Hope Credit, and Lifetime Learning Credit

The most recent tax changes added three new options for education planning. However, it will take some research and/or the advice of some financial advisors to decide which of these options to use and in which order.

## Education IRA/Coverdell Account

An education IRA, more commonly known as a Coverdell account, is a tax-advantaged way to save for educational expenses. A parent or other investor can contribute up to $2,000 after-tax dollars (in 2015), a limit that is reduced if your income is between $95,000 and $110,000 for single people or $190,000 and $220,000 for married couples. Invest the money in nearly any way you like.

People whose adjusted gross incomes (AGIs) are greater than the larger of those two numbers can't use a Coverdell account. Beneficiaries must be younger than 18 to receive account contributions, and they must complete their withdrawals by age 30. Investment income that's still in the account at that point is taxed at the student's regular tax rate, plus a 10 percent penalty. It's possible to name a different account beneficiary within the same family, if the first beneficiary doesn't use all the money. Coverdell accounts typically reduce need-based financial aid awards. You can use them to pay for private elementary and secondary school, as well as college and graduate school.

## 529 Account

A 529 account is much like a Coverdell account, but with a few key differences. Like a Coverdell, a 529 account is a way to save money toward educational expenses. Parents or other investors put in after-tax dollars, use the money to pay educational expenses, and pay taxes plus a 10 percent penalty on any investment income that doesn't go to pay educational fees.

Unlike a Coverdell, however, a 529 account has no contribution limits, and anyone with any income can contribute. Funds can be used only for higher education: college and graduate or professional school. And the investments in a 529 plan are handled by investment managers in the 529 plan of whatever state you choose. All states have 529 accounts, and you don't have to reside in the same state where you invest, though doing so sometimes has state income tax advantages.

You can have both kinds of accounts at the same time, if that makes sense for your situation.

## Hope Credit

The Hope Scholarship Tax Credit, or Hope Credit, provides a $1,500 credit on the family tax return for each student enrolled in postsecondary education. It can only be used for the first two years of enrollment and is available to married couples with AGI up to $100,000 or singles with AGIs up to $50,000.

You cannot use a Hope Credit and a Coverdell account withdrawal or Lifetime Learning Credit in the same year.

## Lifetime Learning Credit

This credit can reduce a family's tax liability by $2,000 each year that a student is enrolled in college, up to four years. Income limits are the same as those of the Hope Credit. Each person in a family can use it, including the parents.

Each of these options has many rules and exceptions attached to them. Please check with a qualified financial advisor before you choose.

## Other Income Tax Deductions and Exemptions

A child who has earned income can take the maximum standard deduction for individuals. This standard deduction reduces the amount of taxable income. Earnings above the deduction amount are taxed at the child's rate, no matter what the child's age.

If a child has income and can be claimed as a dependent on her parents' return, she cannot claim a personal exemption (which is different from a deduction) on her own tax return. If a child cannot be claimed as a dependent, then she can use the standard personal exemption.

## Taxing a Child's Unearned Income

If the money is in the children's names, they pay the taxes on the investment earnings, usually at a lower rate than their parents would pay. However, this is not necessarily an advantage.

You may have heard the phrase *kiddie tax*. Children who are 18 or younger—or who are 23 and younger, if they are full-time students—can receive $1,000 in unearned (investment) income tax free in a given year. The next $1,000 in unearned income is taxed at the child's rate. Unearned income of more than $2,000, however, is taxed at the parents' top marginal tax rate, not the lower capital gains tax that an adult would pay on unearned income. (This rule doesn't apply to earned income, so it's still fine for a kid to have a summer job.)

When a kid receives $9,500 or less in unearned income in a year, parents have the option of reporting that money as part of their own income, which spares the family the kiddie tax. But adding that money to the parents' income can mean that the parents pay more, because they may move to a higher tax bracket or lose out on deductions and credits that phase out as taxpayer income increases.

Your planner can help you figure out the best tax strategy for you. No matter which you choose, you must pay close attention to your children's current unearned income and plan for their future unearned income to decrease the tax bite.

## Income Shifting to Save Taxes

In the past, it usually made sense to shift income from family members in a higher tax bracket to those in a lower tax bracket. The kiddie tax changes this old rule. However, there are still ways to use income-shifting techniques to help you build an education fund.

Before you start, decide whether you're comfortable giving your child control over money. Any monetary gift must be permanent. If you don't want the child to control the money, then income shifting is probably not for you. Come back to this section if and when you are ready to transfer control.

## Will Shifting Save You Taxes?

First, check whether income shifting would provide you any tax advantages. If you're in the same tax bracket, for instance, income shifting will not save you any money.

It's more typical that a child is in a lower tax bracket and a parent is in a higher one. In that case, it may be smart to pursue income shifting. Here are several ways to shift income to your children for their educational or other needs. The first three strategies are only for those who own their own full- or part-time business.

## Use Property to Control Income

If you own a business (a category that includes self-employed people), you can control the amount of income a particular piece of property produces. Consider the equipment you use in your home office. Give it to the children or a trust and rent it back from them. However, this strategy isn't free from IRS challenge, so discuss it with your financial advisors.

## Sideline Business

A second business is an ideal way to shift income to your children. Make them part owners and pay them from the profits.

Use a partnership if the business manages a piece of rental property. Make your children limited partners with no say in management, but they receive a predetermined share of profits.

Use an S corporation if the business is service-oriented and runs without your active involvement. To give your children profits without power, you can issue them nonvoting stock.

## Employ Your Child

Beyond the personal satisfaction of seeing your children learn to function in the working world, there are tax advantages to employing them. First, the kiddie tax applies only to unearned income. They can earn more without having to worry about that rule. Second, they can open a deductible IRA and begin deferring taxes on their income.

Children can take phone calls, file correspondence, deliver documents, check your bookkeeping, or clean the office. Be sure it is useful work, documented by a written record of hours worked and work done. The pay must be reasonable. Don't try to pay a child $20,000 a year for sweeping the floors. Learn what child labor laws apply to your situation.

If your second business is not incorporated, you will not have to pay Social Security taxes or federal unemployment taxes for children under 18 who work for you.

However, if your business is incorporated, you must pay Social Security tax on the wages you pay your children.

If you or someone else pays your child more than $600 per calendar quarter, the child can be considered an employee. The employer should deduct the proper amount from the wages, add an equal amount from his or her own pocket, and then send the total to Social Security. Check with your tax advisor for the proper procedure for determining whether your child is an employee and, if so, how to pay the amount due.

Any child who receives a regular paycheck from an employer will have Social Security tax withheld automatically, just as adults do, and that money is not refundable.

## Loan the Money to Your Child

You can loan your child $10,000 to cover college costs. As long as he or she does not use the income to acquire income-producing property and college tuition is the primary reason for the loan, there may be no income tax consequences. The money is used for college and five years or so later the loan is paid back. You need not charge any interest.

## Second Mortgage/Home Equity Loan

You can take a second mortgage (also called a home equity loan) to cover college costs. In the liability chapter, we'll discuss this option in more detail, including cautions against it. Be forewarned: use the money for college, not to buy a depreciating asset such as a car.

## Avoid Current Taxable Income

Some investments do not produce current taxable income: for example, common stocks, tax-exempt municipal bonds, Series EE bonds, land, certain insurance items, and real estate in which the rental income is equal to or less than the property's holding costs.

If you have growth-oriented investments, you can initially own the investments, then give them to your child after they appreciate. This lets you retain control over the money for a longer time.

Avoid zero coupon bonds. The interest must be reported and the taxes paid yearly at the parents' marginal rate.

## Trusts

Another savings technique involves creating a trust that accumulates income year after year. Trusts must make quarterly estimated tax payments and file tax returns every calendar year. The first portion of trust income is taxed at the rate for the trust's lowest tax bracket.

Trust expenses are subject to the same limitations as those for individuals. Fees for items such as tax preparation, administration, and investment advice are lumped in with miscellaneous charges. Only the portion of the total that is over 2 percent of the trust's AGI is deductible.

Be sure to give the trustee flexibility in distributing income, to take advantage of the best available tax bracket. Either the individual tax rate or the trust tax rate may give you the lowest tax bill, depending on your situation. Check with your tax advisor and attorney to be sure the trust does what you want it to do.

## Gifting: Getting the Money Back to the Child

As of 2015, you may gift up to $14,000 each year to each child. Your spouse may also gift $14,000, giving you a yearly gift total of $28,000 for each child. Gift and invest that money early and your child may have all the funds she needs by the time she is ready for college.

Before you use gifting, discuss it with your financial planner and attorney to be sure you understand how to do it correctly and what the consequences are.

## Conclusion

You can fund your child's education, but it will take disciplined saving and careful strategy. Consider the issue of who controls the money. A successful education plan must coordinate income tax, control, and gift tax considerations.

## Summary

1.  The costs of a college education have been increasing at a faster rate than the rate of inflation. To have enough money to pay these rapidly rising costs, you must plan carefully now.

2.  Determine your needs by finding out the current costs at the actual university your child will probably attend or at similar schools.

3.  Calculate future costs and determine your necessary savings rate using three different funding methods: (1) pay as you go, (2) save each year, and (3) invest a lump sum early.

# CHAPTER 5

# A House Is Not Always a Good Investment

**H**ow many of you think that a house is a good investment? In my seminars, half or more of the class typically raise their hands. If you're like them, here's my next question: Who told you that a house is a good investment? Your banker or your real estate agent, right? And they can't both be wrong, can they?

Your banker and real estate agent are in business to sell mortgages and houses. Of course they're going to tell you to buy your first house or trade up to a larger one. That's how they make their living.

When did this start? Look at newspapers and magazines published before 1950, and try to find a financial expert then who said that a house is a good investment. Only since World War II has the idea of buying a house as an investment been sold to us.

Here's a comparison. I own a Mercedes. Is it a good investment? Every time I've sold a Mercedes since 1970, the car has sold for close to what I paid for it. But it isn't an investment, because of the cost of owning that Mercedes. Every time I drove into a dealership, the manager smiled, because my visits cost at least $500. The cost of owning the car far exceeds the money I recouped when I sold it.

I drive a Mercedes because I can afford it, not because it's a good investment. I own a house because I can afford it, not because it's a good investment.

I want you to understand the difference between real investments, such as a rental property, and personal property, such as a house, a car, or your television. Some things that are real investments, and some things are just ordinary assets. No one would argue that the car you drive every day is an investment.

A house is in the same category. Your home is an ordinary asset, not a real investment. Most people who buy a house spend more on the house than they realize and overextend themselves because they mistakenly think that they are making an investment. Buying too much house is a leading cause of financial stress.

If you happen to buy the right house at the right time in the right place and then sell it at the right time, then you can probably end up with more than the amount of money you originally put into the house. That's a lot of ifs. It's about the same as saying, "Buy low and sell high" in the stock market. Look what happened to people in 1929 or 1987.

A financial decision has two aspects: the economic aspect, which is usually the angle my advice addresses, and the emotional aspect, which is just as valid. Owning a house makes people feel good, but it's not an economically driven investment decision.

I'm not saying that you should never buy a house. I don't rent. I bought a house. However, I don't want you to place your future in a house that you erroneously believe is an investment. I want you to invest for your future with real investments, as I discuss in Chapter 9.

## The True Cost of Home Ownership

How much does a house really cost? Experts say that when you own a house, you spend approximately 1.5 to 2 percent of the cost of the house per month on the mortgage principal and interest, taxes, insurance (sometimes abbreviated as PITI), and maintenance. Maybe that sounds high to you. But unless you do a cash flow worksheet and a balance sheet, you may not realize how much you spend on a house.

### Basic Maintenance and Repair Costs

Remember the cost of the hot water heater you replaced, the roof that you fixed, or the paint for the outside of the house? Those are just some of the basic maintenance and repair costs. What about the extra bathroom you put in or the addition you had built? Don't forget that extra furniture, carpet, and drapes. It all adds up to more money than you realize. As we move from an apartment to a house, we all buy these things.

## Outdoor Living and Transportation

When you buy a house, you'll probably need a lawn mower, a hose, a sprinkler, equipment to fertilize the lawn, a ladder, and garbage cans. You might add a gas grill, deck, patio, or outdoor furniture. Maybe you'll need a second car because you bought that nice house in the suburbs instead of living in an apartment that's close to work.

Of course, these costs aren't money spent directly on the house. However, you probably wouldn't buy those things if you stayed in an apartment. Let's look at a simple example.

## Comparing the Cost: House versus Apartment

Learn more about the housing market in your area. Your local newspaper, real estate agents, and lending institutions are the best sources of current mortgage rates, what parts of town are selling well, the average selling price of a home, and the average number of days a house is on the market before it sells. Use the Internet to search for specific houses and other real estate information. If you don't have a computer at home, your public library can provide Internet access. Ask your planner to recommend loan officers and real estate agents.

That said, bear with me through a hypothetical example. Suppose a house is worth $100,000. You spend $1,500 to $2,000 every month. How does this house compare with an apartment? Table 5.1 shows the comparison between this house and an apartment that rents for $900 per month.

If you found a nice apartment for $900 that was equivalent to a $100,000 house—something you could do in many parts of the country—you would have $600 left over to save and invest. If you could get an 8 percent rate of return on that money, in 20 years your extra money would grow to about $353,000. In 30 years, you would have

| TABLE 5.1 | |
|---|---|

# Buying vs. Renting

| | |
|---|---:|
| Value of the house | $100,000 |
| Principal, interest, taxes, insurance, and maintenance/month | × .015 |
| Extra cost of the house | 1,500 |
| Equivalent apartment | − 900 |
| Extra cash | $600 |

around $894,000. Think what you could do with that money! Is your house really worth that loss of savings?

I'm convinced that the number-one reason most people today are behind the financial eight ball is because they live beyond their means, usually by owning more house than they should. When you can't save any money, your house is one of the places to look. Do you really need to have a $150,000 house when a $100,000 house may do fine? The difference in the mortgage and upkeep costs could be money to save for your retirement. Can you afford to own and maintain an expensive house? Will you reach financial freedom if you spend a large part of your money on that house? You need to think seriously about these questions. The true cost of a house may be that you never reach financial independence.

## Valid Reasons for Owning a House

Don't go out and immediately sell your house. There are perfectly valid reasons for owning a house. Buy a house because you like it, because it is a comfortable place to live, because you want a yard for the kids to play in, because you want pets and the landlord won't let you have them, or because your hobby is ham radio and you can't put an antenna up in an apartment. But don't buy a house solely as a real investment and don't buy more house than you can afford.

## Living beyond Your Means

How many couples do you know in which both partners are working so they can afford a nice house? It all gets back to that obstacle—ego—that

I talked about in the first chapter. People try to satisfy their egos and end up depleting their savings. They are never going to reach their true goals if they must scrimp and save to pay for a house that's beyond their means.

Look at it another way. An expensive car is a joy to have, if you can afford it, and many luxury cars have appreciated over time. Would you send your wife to work to support a Mercedes Benz? Would you ask your husband to work a second job for a Porsche? If you wouldn't do it for a car, why do it for a house?

## A House as an Investment

I'm familiar with many of the counterarguments, which typically involve interest deductions and an inflation hedge.

### The Interest Deduction Argument

"But what about the tax deduction for interest?" someone always asks in my seminars.

Interest is an expense, not a deduction. If you want to rationalize paying interest on a real estate purchase, buy a rental property.

When you own your home, you can deduct the interest you pay on the mortgage. With a rental property, you can also deduct depreciation and maintenance costs. When the plumber does work on your rental property, the repair cost is deductible.

When you own your home, its market value may appreciate. Even if you are willing and able to sell it for the appreciated price, what do you do? You buy another house to live in and your money is tied up again. When you sell a rental property, there is no urgency to find another place to live, so you are able to make an informed economic decision, not an emotional decision.

Based on these three factors, the smart investor would buy a house or apartment to rent to someone else. If you buy a duplex, you can live in one side and deduct the other. Better yet, buy a multiple-unit building. Of course, you must consider whether you want to be a landlord and who would do the maintenance and repairs. I discuss real estate as an investment in Chapter 9.

## Owning a House Is Not a Hedge against Inflation

Over the long term, a house's increase in value barely keeps up with inflation. Suppose you bought an existing home in 1986 for the national average price of $80,300. Figure 5.1 shows what happened from 1986 to 1997 to existing home prices. It also shows you how that $80,300 would have increased if you had invested it in six-month Treasury bills or long-term government securities. By 1997, you would have had between $24,000 and $59,000 more than the average house would have been worth by investing in either of those two products. Imagine what you

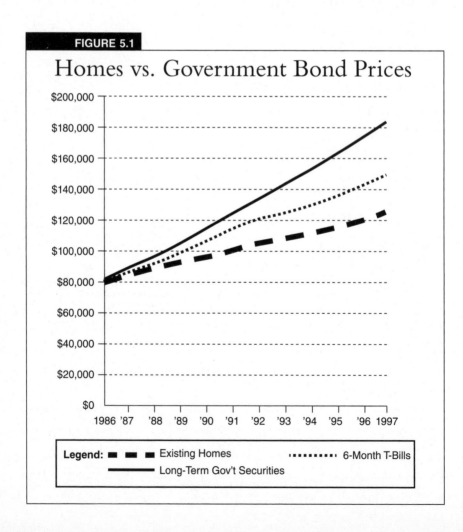

FIGURE 5.1

**Homes vs. Government Bond Prices**

Legend: ■ ■ ■ Existing Homes    •••••••••• 6-Month T-Bills
————— Long-Term Gov't Securities

might have earned if you had invested in the stock market during the same period.

If you had sold this hypothetical house by 1988, you might have made the same return on it as on the other investments. But when most people sell their house, they buy another house. The money is tied up again. In 1990, the rate of increase for existing home prices was 2.9 percent. Six-month Treasury bills (T-bills) were earning 0.5 percent, and long-term government securities were at 0.6 percent. Figure 5.2 compares home value inflation compared to investment interest.

When you buy government debt, you know ahead of time what rate of return you will get and when you will get it. That's peace of mind. When you buy a house, no one can predict what your rate of return will be or how quickly you will be able to sell your house. In the late 1970s, most people would have said that buying a house in Houston or Dallas was a good investment. Then oil prices went down and the housing market followed. Since then, Houston's housing market has strongly

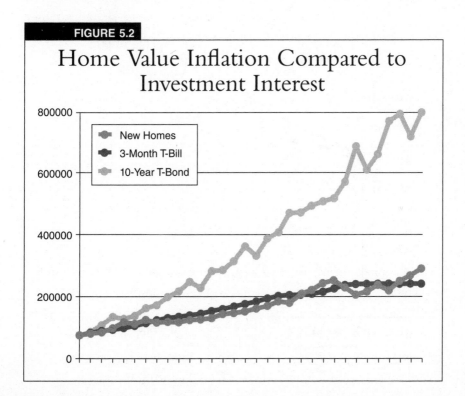

**FIGURE 5.2**

Home Value Inflation Compared to Investment Interest

Legend:
- New Homes
- 3-Month T-Bill
- 10-Year T-Bond

recovered. There's no way of knowing during which part of the cycle you might be buying or selling.

Can a house be a real investment? Sure, if you treat the buy/sell decision as an economic one. For example, I know one client who sold his personal residence when market values were rising after a slump of four or five years. He planned to rent until the real estate market settled back down. When the prices declined again, he planned to buy another house. He made economic decisions, not emotional decisions about that particular house. Most of us can't do that, because owning our personal residence is an emotional decision. That's perfectly acceptable. Just be honest with yourself about your reasons for owning a house and about how much house you can afford.

## Buy Now or Buy Later

The next argument that usually comes up relates not so much to a home's so-called investment value as to the timing of the purchase. We've all been told to buy a house as soon as you can or when interest rates are low. Not true. Even if you wait to buy a house, you will still come out ahead because of compound interest (see Figure 5.3).

Consider an example that compares two possible scenarios. In both cases, instead of buying a house immediately, you wait 10 years. You put the down payment into savings immediately. Each month you save an amount of money equivalent to the mortgage payment. Under assumption A you earn a 7 percent rate of return and experience 5 percent inflation. You would only need $1,181 more to buy the house. The mortgage on a house bought today would still have $42,873 outstanding. Your total savings would be $41,692. Under assumption B's higher rates, you would save $17,410.

Of course, during those 10 years, you would have to pay rent to live somewhere else. The difference in overhead comes from all the money you didn't have to pay for taxes, insurance, and all those maintenance and repair costs on a house. However, if you stayed in the same house the entire time, chances are you would be living well below your means. Every situation is different and must be individually addressed.

| FIGURE 5.3 | | |
|---|---|---|

## Compound Interest

| | | |
|---|---|---|
| 1. Cost of house today | $100,000 | |
| 2. Down payment | 20,000 | |
| 3. Mortgage | 80,000 | |
| 4. Interest | 10% | |
| 5. Length of loan | 30 years | |
| 6. Monthly payment | $702 | |
| | | |
| — But if you wait 10 years | *Assumption A* | *Assumption B* |
| 7. Invest that money at | 7% | 8% |
| 8. Inflation | 5% | 7% |
| 9. Future cost of house | $162,889 | $196,715 |
| 10. Invest monthly payment | 121,515 | 128,439 |
| 11. Invest down payment | 40,193 | 44,393 |
| 12. Total available to buy | $161,709 | $172,831 |
| 13. Would still owe (#9–#12) | $1,181 | $ 23,884 |
| | | |
| — If you had bought the house | | |
| 14. Tax bracket | 30% | 30% |
| 15. Mortgage balance after 10 years | $72,750 | $72,750 |
| 16. Invest tax savings from interest deduction | 29,877 | 31,456 |
| 17. Mortgage balance left | $42,873 | $41,294 |

*Source:* US Bureau of Census from 1984 to January 2015

Be sure to evaluate what compound interest can do for you. Don't rush out now and buy a house that you may not be able to afford. By waiting, you may be able to save more money and still buy a house, if that's one of your goals.

## Making the Most Use of Your Cash Flow

If you decide to buy a house—and most of you will—then you can make the most of your cash flow by putting less down on the house. Using credit to increase your buying power is a form of leverage, the same principle people use in investment real estate. This can be dangerous when the market goes down. You can end up underwater, owing more than the house is worth. However, in a home purchase, using a lower down payment allows you to make better use of your cash flow. The most efficient use of your cash is to invest it rather than to tie up the money in your house. For example, if your mortgage payment would be $700 with one house but you can lower that to $500 by purchasing a less expensive house, you can invest the $200 difference toward reaching your goal. If you will spend that $200, however, then you should not do this.

Managing inflation can be an additional benefit of leveraging your home. If you live in your home for an extended period, the mortgage payment will become less and less a portion of your cash flow. Inflation is a friend to fixed interest, and will reduce the real cost of these payments over time.

If you decide to use leverage in buying your house, you will probably want to make the down payment enough to avoid being required to escrow your taxes and insurance. A 20 percent down payment is usually sufficient. You must balance this against other financial factors, such as existing debt or whether you've met your goals for saving and investing. If you've met your goal, you don't have to worry about using your cash flow efficiently. Here's where a financial advisor can help you look at different scenarios and choose your best strategy.

## Shopping for a Mortgage

It's funny that people will spend more time choosing clothes or discussing the latest sports game than selecting a mortgage company. There are many useful books on how to buy (or sell) your house. Spend some time at your public library and then shop around for a mortgage. There are many mortgage resources online, including mortgage calculators (Bankrate), as well as reputable mortgage brokers who can present you with a number of options from lenders competing for your business.

### Land Contract, Purchase Money Agreement, or Deed for Contract

In these arrangements, the seller finances the mortgage. In land contracts and deeds for contract, the seller keeps the title until the buyer pays the full purchase amount. In a purchase money agreement, the seller finances the mortgage but the buyer receives the title. When the real estate market is not good and interest rates are high, making properties more difficult to sell, these mortgages are popular. They can also be dangerous, as a buyer who misses a payment can forfeit the property without any equity.

## Biweekly Mortgage

By making payments every two weeks instead of once a month, the buyer effectively makes 13 monthly payments. If the two payments equaled a normal monthly payment, a 30-year mortgage would be paid off in 21 years. This method, of course, means giving up some other potential investment opportunities.

## Graduated Payment Mortgage

Set up for first-time homeowners, these mortgage payments begin at a lower rate. Then they increase until reaching a payment that stays the same for the rest of the loan. We don't like these.

## Closing Costs

Closing costs can be overwhelming. Here's a brief definition of each term.

## Application Fee

Collected when you apply for a mortgage, this fee covers loan-processing costs. It is nonrefundable unless the lender turns down your application. This fee can be negotiated or even waived.

## Appraisal Fee

A professional appraiser works for the lender and determines the home's market value. The lender wants to know that the property is worth at least the loan amount. The appraiser uses the selling prices of comparable properties and a physical home inspection to establish the home's value. You will still need to hire your own inspector, who will give you a detailed report on the home's condition.

## Credit Report Fee

The lender orders a detailed credit report from one or more of the credit-reporting companies. This report shows all credit transactions you have made for the last seven years, if you paid on time or were late, and other credit risk factors that may concern the lender. You're entitled to a free, annual copy of your credit report from each credit-reporting company, just for the asking, and can point out errors or add explanations to your file. Contact the three major credit bureaus at equifax.com, experian.com, and transunion.com.

## Loan Origination Fee

The bank or mortgage company that originates the loan keeps this fee as part of its profit.

## Discount Fee (Points)

A point is 1 percent of the mortgage amount. Paying it reduces the loan's interest rate. This fee increases the lender's total profit. The seller pays points for VA and FHA loans. The buyer pays the points for a conventional mortgage. On a new mortgage, points can be deducted from your income tax return for the year the loan began. When refinancing, you must deduct the points over the life of the loan. Points can be negotiated. Generally, the lower the interest rate you want, the more points you pay. However, in a highly competitive market, it is not unusual for lenders to waive points or offer you a better mortgage rate in the first place.

## Processing Fee

This fee covers the lender's processing costs and overhead. Again, its rate can be negotiated.

## Mortgage Title Insurance

This special type of insurance covers both buyer and lender. It ensures that the seller has clear title to the property and that the title is properly transferred, without liens or encumbrances.

## Prepaid Interest

At closing, the buyer prepays the interest from the closing date to the date of the first mortgage payment.

## Mortgage Insurance

Lenders typically try to sell borrowers mortgage insurance in the form of a declining-benefit term life insurance policy that pays your mortgage off if you die before paying it off yourself. It's a product that benefits the lender much more than it benefits you, and you're not required to buy it. If you need insurance to cover your mortgage, make that choice based on your whole financial plan and choose a better product.

## Private Mortgage Insurance

If your down payment is less than 20 percent of the home's selling price, the lender usually requires that you pay for private mortgage insurance (PMI). As soon as you have 20 percent equity in the house, ask the lender to remove this insurance. This may be a warning sign that you cannot afford the house.

## Recording Fees

The county or town where your home is located charges a fee to record the deed and mortgage.

## Prepaid Property Taxes

Property taxes are usually paid ahead, so the buyer reimburses the seller on a prorated basis for taxes already paid on the property.

## Escrow Reserve for Property Taxes

Next year's taxes go into an escrow account, to make sure that they will be paid. Depending on your down payment amount, you may be able to avoid this. Be sure to ask, especially if you can earn more interest on the money than the escrow account is paying.

### Escrow Reserve for Hazard and Flood Insurance

As with the property tax escrow, money for hazard and flood insurance goes into an escrow account. Find out how big a down payment you'll need to avoid escrow, and consider making that down payment. You should set aside the money you'll need to pay the insurance bill when it arrives. Your cash flow worksheet can help you plan for this expense.

### Real Estate Transfer Tax/Revenue Stamps

Property transfers are taxable transactions.

## Saving Money on Your Mortgage

Whether you have a mortgage now or are looking for your first home, you can save money on a mortgage by reducing your monthly payment or reducing your total liability. Use some or all of these methods:

### Reduce Your Payment

Can you reduce or eliminate tax or insurance escrow costs? Can you refinance at a lower rate or shop around for a better rate for your new mortgage? With a larger down payment—usually 20 percent or more—you can typically avoid extra costs, such as private mortgage insurance and some escrows. However, you will have to weigh this against the advantages of putting down a smaller down payment and having more money to invest. Consider the closing costs on a refinance.

### Reduce Your Total Liability

Can you increase your monthly payment? A 15-year mortgage costs less than a 30-year mortgage in total interest paid. Can you make a large payment in the future, perhaps when a certificate of deposit matures?

Whatever your strategy, keep the big picture in mind. Consider carefully before making a decision that might save money on your mortgage but would cost you financially in another way.

## How Much Can You Afford?

Home purchasers often hear that they can afford a house that costs two and one-half to three times their gross incomes. That should be your maximum. Focus on what amount you can really handle. Go back to your cash flow worksheet and look at these three amounts:

**1.** How much do you have for a down payment?

**2.** How much do you have for a monthly payment?

**3.** What other debts do you have?

## Ratios to Calculate

Next, figure out these two ratios:

**1.** Mortgage Payment/Monthly Gross Income. This ratio should be 28 percent or less.

**2.** Overall Debt/Monthly Gross Income. This ratio should be 36 percent or less.

Lenders usually say that you can afford the smaller of these two numbers. As an example, suppose your monthly gross income is $4,000. The ratios listed above are calculated as:

**1.** 28 percent × 4,000 = $1,200 maximum monthly payment

**2.** 36 percent × 4,000 = $1,440 maximum overall monthly debt payments

Subtract monthly payments on other debts from this maximum. If your car payment is $500 and your credit card payment is $100, subtract $600 from your maximum house payment. The result is a maximum monthly house payment of $840. In this example, a lender would allow the smaller number: a monthly house payment of $840.

Once you have these numbers, you're ready to talk to a mortgage lender and a Realtor. Remember that both make more money when you spend more money, and don't let them talk you into more house than you want. You know your circumstances and level of financial discipline. Don't let ego get in the way of sound financial decision making.

## Refinancing an Existing Mortgage

Should you refinance an existing mortgage? You can usually save money if (1) the new rate will be at least 2 percent below your current rate, and (2) you keep the house for the number of months it takes to recover the closing costs. Figure 5.4 shows an easy example of how to calculate this break-even point. Don't worry about the actual rates used in this example. Just focus on how to calculate your possible savings.

Remember that the monthly payment savings will be offset by the lump-sum closing costs until you reach the break-even point. In the example in Figure 5.4, you would have to keep the house almost two years to benefit from refinancing.

## Paying Off the Mortgage Early

Along with the myth of a house as an investment, you may have heard that you should prepay your mortgage. Build up your equity and save

---

**FIGURE 5.4**

# Calculating Break-Even Point

Example: Suppose you refinance a house worth $100,000 at a new rate of 8 percent

| | |
|---|---|
| Current monthly payment at 9.5% | $840.85 |
| Proposed monthly payment at 8% | −733.76 |
| Monthly pretax savings | 107.09 |
| 1.00 − 0.30 (tax bracket) | ×0.70 |
| Monthly after-tax savings | 74.96 |
| Lost investment return | −10.00* |
| Net monthly savings | 64.96 |
| Total refinancing cost | $1,500.00 |

**Months to break even ($1,500/$64.96) = 23 months**

*$1,500 × .08 return = $120 per year/12 months = $10 per month.

thousands of dollars in interest, the experts cry. Consider these four points before you pay ahead on your mortgage.

1.  Are you meeting your goals? If not, why tie up more money in your house when that money should be put toward meeting your goals?

2.  If you are meeting your goals, how does the interest rate on your mortgage compare with what you could earn in a different investment? Remember to factor in the effect of taxes on your mortgage interest rate. If you are in a 25 percent federal tax bracket and an 8 percent state tax bracket, and your mortgage rate is 4.5 percent, then your after-tax mortgage rate is 3.105 percent. (Do the math at www.bankrate.com/calculators/mortgages/loan-tax-deduction-calculator.aspx.) If you can find a tax-free investment earning 4 percent, why prepay your mortgage?

3.  Are you sure that your house will continue to appreciate at a rate that's at or above the rate of inflation? This assumption is one of the cornerstones of the prepayment advice. If you own a home in a good location and homes like yours are selling at appreciated prices, it's hard to imagine that it won't always be that way. But the housing market has cycles, just like any other investment. Recall the plunging housing market in Texas when oil prices fell, not to mention the subprime mortgage crisis, when the bottom dropped out of many housing markets. There are no guarantees when you have money tied up in your house. When you put your money in a certificate of deposit, your rate is guaranteed.

4.  Consider liquidity. A house is not a liquid asset, but a T-bill is. Don't tie up money that you might need for emergencies.

There some advantages to prepaying. First, if you can't save any other way, perhaps prepaying will force you to save something. Second, if you only intend to stay in the house for a few years, you might want to build equity faster (but consider interest rates, as I mentioned earlier). Finally, if you have excess cash flow and have considered all these points, you may want to prepay.

## Home Equity Loans

A home equity loan is a second mortgage. There may be valid reasons for having one, such as education costs, business capital, or financial hardship, but remember that failure to repay means you could lose your home

Interest on a home equity loan is tax deductible, up to certain limits. No other consumer loan interest is tax deductible, which makes home equity loans very enticing as an extra source of cash. Don't ever use a home equity loan to pay for a depreciating asset, such as a car, furniture, or a vacation. It's not worth the risk.

# Buying and Selling

Whether you are buying or selling a home, remember that this is a financial transaction. It's okay to buy a home for emotional reasons, but try to keep your emotions in control during the process. Falling in love with the house before you've thoroughly checked it out is a mistake. When you sell, it's hard to be objective about the strong and weak points of a home that has so many memories. There are many good books and magazine articles on this subject, so I'll just mention the main points of buying and selling.

## Buying a House

Real estate agents say the three most important things about a house are location, location, and location. You may never sell your home, but someone eventually will, and its location will help or hinder that sale.

Start following mortgage rates and home prices before you buy, to get a feel for the market. Then you will know when rates are good and how one house compares with another. Have a lender preapprove you, so you'll know how much house you can afford.

Have a home inspection. In fact, consider having two inspections: one by a professional home inspector and one by a licensed structural engineer. It's worth the extra cost to know whether that ceiling crack is cosmetic or indicates structural damage.

## Selling a House

Whether you decide to use a real estate agent or sell the house yourself, do the less expensive things first before putting your home on the market.

Get the clutter out of the house. Clean out the closets, have a yard sale, or donate unused stuff to a charity. Repair all those small things you've ignored: the leaky faucet, the squeaky hinges, the torn window screen. Clean up inside and outside. If washing the walls doesn't improve their looks, paint them a neutral color.

If the house has problems, don't cover them up. Be honest about what you've done to fix the issues. Get a repair estimate as a basis for negotiation.

## Home Improvements

Before you add a hot tub or any other improvement to a house, do your homework, especially if you hope the improvement will help you sell or sell for a higher price. Some improvements will return 100 percent of their cost, or close to it, in the home's eventual sales price; others may actually make it harder to sell the house. Several magazines offer yearly surveys of the value of home improvements when selling a home. Check out your local library for the latest research.

When you buy a home, don't guess at the cost of home improvements. Check the magazine articles at your library for average costs of typical improvements. Then talk to local contractors to see what the price range is in your area.

## What Taxes Will Be Due from Your Home Sale?

Check with your tax advisor for the latest laws regarding the exclusion of profits from the sale of your home. The current exclusion for married joint filers is up to $500,000 and $250,000 for single filers. This exclusion can be used once every two years. If you have been deferring profits from previous sales, check to see whether those profits plus your current gain will exceed the exclusion. You will owe tax on the amount above that.

# Summary

You should own a house because you want one and can afford it, not because it's a good investment. Your home is an ordinary asset, not a real investment. Owning one is an emotional decision, not an investment decision.

A house is the biggest expenditure you will ever have. Most of us don't know the true cost of a house. Every month you spend 1.5 to 2 percent of your house's value on mortgage principal, interest, taxes, insurance, and maintenance. However, unless you do a cash flow worksheet and a balance sheet, you may not realize all that you spend on the house. For the same cost, many of us could live in a very nice apartment and still have money left to save.

If you don't currently own a house, carefully evaluate whether to buy one now or wait until you can better afford it. If you already own a house, how can you cut costs? Is a move to a less expensive house necessary to have more money for savings and thus meet your goal of financial independence?

If you already own a house, this doesn't mean you should immediately sell it. There are very good emotional reasons to own a house. Buy a house because you want a yard for the kids or a big garden, but don't buy a house as an investment. Too many two-income households try to support a house they can't afford. Remember that one of the obstacles to achieving financial independence is ego. Don't satisfy your ego with a house and risk your long-term goals.

# CHAPTER 6

# Insurance

When you're just starting out, you usually have few investments, but you still need insurance. Insurance fills the gap between what you have and what you need to protect your loved ones.

As your investments grow, your need for insurance decreases. However, most investors are still somewhere in the insurance-gap years.

In this chapter, you'll learn about the two types of life insurance and their variations, the two types of insurance companies, how agents earn their money, tax considerations, why you need disability insurance, and how to find and evaluate the best buys in insurance.

Review your cash flow and spendable cash worksheets. These will help you identify how much you currently spend on insurance, as well as how any given insurance policy premium will affect your spendable cash.

Consider hypothetical scenarios. If you die, how does that affect your spouse, children, or any other dependents? What happens if you're the victim of a burglary? A serious accident? Make a list of realistic possibilities and note the likely financial effect of each one.

## Types of Life Insurance

If you're like many people, your death would be disastrous, not just to you, but to the people who rely on you. Your dependents may rely on you for financial support, and if you're the primary caregiver for a child, a person with disability, or an elderly person, your contribution would be expensive to replace.

Life insurance can't keep you alive, of course, but it can soften the financial blow to the people you leave behind. Life insurance seems to come in as many varieties as ice cream these days, but the names are not much help in describing what they will do for you.

There are only two types of insurance: term and cash value.

## Term Life Insurance

Term insurance pays a death benefit if you die within the period that the policy is in effect—its term. If you buy a 20-year term life insurance policy, you and the issuer are essentially making opposing bets. You bet that you will die within that 20 years. The insurance company bets that you will stay alive. (I realize this may sound a bit crass, but that's what insurance boils down to.)

Term life insurance sets a single price for coverage during the policy's entire term. You cannot reduce the coverage—and the cost of that coverage—as your investments gain value and you need less insurance. You're stuck with the coverage you initially selected, unless you want to take a loss on all you paid so far, so you keep paying for a product that doesn't fit you as well as it used to.

## Credit Life Insurance

Avoid credit life, which is also called decreasing term insurance. It's the most expensive kind of life insurance and gives you no control over the value of the insurance. The protection decreases each year, whether or not you want it to. This is the type of insurance you are offered when you take out a car loan or mortgage, for example. It's better to plan your entire insurance coverage. Buy one-policy, piecemeal coverage for each loan you take out.

## Cash Value or Whole Life Insurance

Cash value life insurance is sold by many names: whole life, single-premium whole life, universal life, variable life, and many hybrid forms. Let's look at the specific details of the four main types of cash value insurance: whole life, universal life, variable life, and single premium.

## Whole Life

Whole life policy owners pay a fixed premium on regular payment dates in order to receive a death benefit that you fix when you buy the policy.

You cannot make investment choices and have no guaranteed rate of return on the policy's cash value. You may take out a loan against the policy at a fixed or variable interest rate.

## Universal Life

Universal life policyholders choose an initial death benefit that you can raise or lower each year. The premium can be fixed or variable, an amount that you can periodically increase or reduce, or even skip occasionally. You cannot make investment choices but generally get a guaranteed minimum rate of return on the policy's cash value. Any return above that minimum varies. The rate the agent quotes to you will probably be the rate before costs are deducted. You can make partial withdrawals by paying a fee and interest.

If you do not pay enough in premiums to cover the cost of insuring you, either the company will subtract what you owe from your policy's cash value or the policy will lapse.

## Variable Life

When you buy the policy, you choose the initial death benefit and pay a fixed or variable premium periodically. You can select stock, bond, and money market portfolios—investment choices look like mutual funds—and adjust your choice by contacting the company. Investment performance determines the rate of return. If the investments you choose do well, your death benefit may increase. This type of insurance policy charges two fees—a mortality and expense charge and an investment management expense—that other types of life insurance do not.

## Single Premium Adjustable Whole Life

As with whole life, the death benefit in this policy type is fixed when you buy the policy. The premium is a lump sum payment of anywhere from $5,000 to $1 million. You have no investment choices. The rate of return on the cash value is generally guaranteed and typically changes every one to three years. You can borrow against equity, usually at a modest interest rate, or against earnings for zero interest.

A single-premium whole life policy is not appropriate for short-term needs (for less than 10 years). Cashing it in early costs you part of the premium, so that you lose 9 percent the first year, 8 percent the second year, and so forth. If surrender charges continue more than seven years, don't buy the policy.

If you like the loan privileges that come with this type of insurance, find a policy that guarantees a rate of zero on loans against your earnings and no more than 2 percent on loans against your original premium.

## Single Premium Variable Life

As a policyholder, you choose the death benefit when you purchase the policy. The death benefit may increase if the investments do well but will not drop below a base amount. You pay a lump sum premium of from $5,000 to $1 million and choose among stock, bond, and money market portfolios, changing your choice by contacting the company. There is no guaranteed rate of return. You can borrow against equity, usually at a modest interest rate, or against earnings for zero interest.

Buy this policy for long-term coverage. Most of the premium covers expenses during the first 10 years that the policy is in effect. If you borrow against your policy, the best return the issuer will give you is one equal to your loan interest. If you choose stock investments, don't borrow much against the policy, as doing so could mean that you lose a lot in a volatile equities market.

## Hybrid Policies

There are many different variations on cash value life insurance, and every year a new one seems to appear. Current contenders include:

**Modified life.** This is a whole life policy with a lower premium in the early years.

**Limited payment life.** You pay premiums for a limited number of years on a whole life policy.

**Family income.** This policy combines decreasing term and whole life insurance.

**Adjustable life.** This lets you switch between term and cash value insurance.

# My Recommendation

In general, term life insurance is the best buy. Because the marketplace is so fluid, I can't recommend a specific type of term insurance. The best buy today will probably not be the best buy tomorrow. Do your homework and compare policies.

To compare term with cash value policies, find the best buy in term insurance. Then ask the agent for a comparison of that term policy with a cash value policy. Be aware that a particular company's term policy will not compare favorably with its own cash value policy.

You can also ask your planner to evaluate whether you have the best value for your life insurance dollar by using the National Association of Insurance Commissioners' interest-adjusted net payment cost index and surrender cost index, which both aid in comparing costs. Your planner can use these indexes to make an apples-to-apples comparison of different policies.

Remember: you want to buy basic protection, not make an investment. Do your tax sheltering with tools, not insurance.

Life insurance premiums are based on standard mortality tables, which are available online. (See www.pbgc.gov/prac/mortality-retirement-and-pv-max-guarantee/erisa-mortality-tables/erisa-section-4050-mortality-table-for-2015-valuation-dates.html for an example.) Other risk factors, such as smoking and illness, also help determine your premium.

Your best insurance may be available through your membership in a social association such as the Elks Club, the Optimists, or through the national organization for your profession. If that organization also offers term insurance, it will probably offer good rates (because of the large member pool) and may also offer additional coverage that you might not find in an individual policy.

If you don't already belong to a professional association, check to see what is available for your business and related businesses. Some professional associations have less strict membership requirements—support of their aims, interest in the field, and so on—than others that require professional licensure. It may pay to investigate.

## Types of Insurance Companies

There are two types of insurance companies: the sort that pays dividends and the sort that is known as participating, or par.

If your insurance company pays dividends, you can do five things with those dividends.

1. Take cash.
2. Use them to reduce your premiums. This is the best option.
3. Let them accumulate with the company.
4. Purchase additional cash value insurance. If you are under 45, a dividend-paying policy may be cheaper.
5. Purchase one-year term insurance.

## Tax Considerations

Life insurance does not go through probate. It is subject to federal estate taxes and may be subject to state estate taxes, depending on the state. For example, life insurance benefits are not taxed by the state of Ohio if the insurance is properly set up and the beneficiary is not the insured person's estate.

### Tax Shelter

Life insurance is sometimes sold as a tax shelter. There are some advantages to this, including:

1. Earnings on cash value grow tax deferred.
2. You can borrow the earnings from the policy tax free. The interest is tax deductible.

3. The beneficiary gets policy proceeds free of federal income tax.

4. The premium is generally fixed when you take out the policy and does not increase.

   The disadvantages include:

5. You get a decent return only after holding the policy for several years.

6. The insurance company makes all investment decisions (variable life policies are the exception).

7. This product suffers from a lack of liquidity. You can only get the money out as a loan. Generally you can't take out as much as you put in for a considerable time; single-premium life is the exception.

8. The death benefit is usually fixed at the policy's beginning and does not adjust for inflation. What sounds like a lot of money when you take out a policy may be chicken feed by the time the policy pays a death benefit.

## How Insurance Agents Earn Money

Insurance agents are paid a percentage of the premiums on the policies they sell. They are not paid by the number of policies they sell and have no financial incentive to find the best policy for you. They make more money if you buy a whole life policy than if you buy term insurance. You should buy insurance to protect you, not to pay someone else's commission.

## Common Sales Pitches

Here are the seven most common sales pitches that agents use to sell life insurance:

1. **Life insurance gives peace of mind without risk.** The U.S. government does not insure life insurance policies. Most states have guaranty funds that pay claims and continue coverage if an insurance company is declared insolvent. Some states, including California, New Jersey, and Ohio, have no such funds. Check with your state

insurance commissioner to see if your state has a guaranty fund. If your insurer goes out of business, you or your beneficiaries might not receive everything you paid for.

2. **If you buy term insurance, all you have to show for it are receipts, like renting instead of buying a house.** But if home prices are too high and rents are reasonable, why not rent? Likewise, why pay too much for whole life when term insurance will meet your goal?

3. **Sell your municipal bonds and buy single-premium whole life so your earnings will be automatically reinvested.** You can invest in municipal bond mutual funds, which also reinvest automatically, don't have all the extra charges, and have more liquidity. Take your savings and buy term insurance.

4. **Loans against a single-premium policy's cash value have zero net interest, and there are no federal income taxes on the loan.** Don't borrow most of the cash value or you will no longer have a policy. In addition, you will owe tax on the difference between what you paid in premiums and what you borrowed. Not all insurance companies warn you that you are about to borrow too much.

5. **Life insurance is a tax shelter, plus you earn double-digit interest rates.** No company can guarantee double-digit rates. The high initial rates you hear quoted is usually before expenses are deducted; it may only be good for a year or a month. It's a teaser intended to sell you a policy. Not all companies will divulge policy expenses unless you specifically ask.

   When you look at policies, forget those that quote a rate much higher than current rates on Treasury bonds or quality corporate bonds. Higher rates mean higher risk.

6. **The insurance is free because this is such a fantastic investment.** You don't get something for nothing. Insurance companies are in business to make money, so somewhere there is a charge to

cover the payout and the company's profit. This charge will come out of your fantastic investment, if the charge is not shown elsewhere. How good an investment is it, really? Do your investing elsewhere unless this is the only way you can discipline yourself to save.

# Disability Insurance

Everyone needs disability insurance. In middle age, you're more likely to become disabled than to die.

Even if your company provides you with some disability insurance, don't be lulled into a false sense of security. Based on my experience, you will probably still need to get your own policy. Most company disability policies either don't have enough coverage or are too limited by their restrictions.

What do you need? Look for insurance that cannot be canceled and is guaranteed renewable with an inflation rider, provision for partial residual benefits, and an "own occupation" definition of disability. That's a mouthful, isn't it. Let's define the terms.

## Noncancelable

The policy can never be canceled, regardless of your circumstances, as long as you pay the premiums. A change in your health or job might cause some policies to be canceled if they do not have this provision. This feature also guarantees the premium and benefit amount.

## Guaranteed Renewable

At the policy renewal date, the company must allow you to buy the policy again until you reach a certain age, such as age 65.

## Inflation Rider

This gives you some protection against inflation by annually increasing the benefit while you are disabled. The increase can be calculated with either compound or simple interest and can be guaranteed or tied to the consumer price index (CPI).

## Partial Residual Benefits

These can be either an integral part of the policy or added as a rider. This provision will pay a reduced benefit based on the insured's percentage of income loss. For example, a physician earning $10,000 per month who suffers a 50 percent loss of income would receive 50 percent of the monthly benefit stated in the policy. Note that some policies require a period of total disability to qualify for this benefit. A rider can usually eliminate this requirement.

## Own Occupation

This definition of disability means you'll get your benefits if you're unable to work in your own occupation, even if you're earning income from a different occupation. One of my clients, for instance, is a dentist with a bum shoulder whose disability policy has funded his lifestyle for 35 years.

Some policies have an "own occupation" definition of disability for only the first year or two of disability. After that, they have an "any occupation" definition. For example, a physician who is unable to perform surgery but can teach would collect full disability benefits for two years. Thereafter, other earned income would reduce or eliminate the benefits.

## Understanding Terminology

As you can see, disability insurance is an area where you can really lose if you don't understand the terms. Check your company policy to see if it covers all five areas and be careful when making future purchases.

Finally, one more point to help you find a policy. With disability insurance, expensive is often better. Shop by benefits offered, not premium price.

## How to Evaluate Insurance Companies and Policies

Here are three ways to evaluate both companies and policies before you buy:

1. Go to your library and check the reports of the insurance rating agencies, including Weiss Research (www.weissratings.com), Duff & Phelps (www.dcroo.com), Moodys (www.moodys.com), Standard and Poor's (www.standardandpoor.com), and A. Best (www.ambest .com/index.html). Look at more than one report; some agencies go easier in their ratings than others.

2. Write to the Insurance Forum, Inc., P.O. Box 245, Ellettsville, IN 47429, or call 812-876-6502 for information on its newsletter, edited by Joseph Belth, former insurance commissioner of Pennsylvania. A few issues each year are devoted to the consumer. Back issues are available. The calculations are useful but take time to complete. See if your library has this newsletter.

3. Check with your state's insurance commissioner to see if there is state backing for insurance companies. Several companies will provide you with a list of insurance policies that meet your specifications (age, sex, amount, and so forth). Check recent issues of consumer magazines for the details or ask your reference librarian.

## The ABC Technique

Use this technique to help you evaluate any business proposal. It will help you decide which insurance policy to buy, which investments to purchase, and how to answer some of the other questions you will have in implementing your financial plan. This works for oil wells, real estate, insurance, or anything you need to compare.

Let's say that you need disability insurance. Call Agent A and say that you need disability insurance and would like to see a proposal. Tell Agents B and C the same thing.

Now you have three proposals. Go to Agent B and say that, while you were waiting for Agent B's proposal, you received Agent A's proposal. Would Agent B mind telling me what's wrong with Agent A's proposal? Go to Agent C and show her Agent B's proposal, and to Agent A with Agent C's proposal. You'll learn which is the best proposal.

You're not doing this to embarrass people or to take advantage of them. You're trying to learn.

It's your money. No one cares as much about your money as you do. I manage my clients' money. Many times I lose sleep over it. But I still don't care as much about their money as they do.

## Summary

1. Buy life insurance for protection, not for investment. Term insurance should give you the best value for your dollar. Take the time to evaluate policies and shop for the best buy.

2. For your other insurance needs—health, disability, homeowner's or renter's insurance, automobile, personal liability, and professional and malpractice coverage—take the same care in evaluating and choosing policies.

3. There are only two basic types of life insurance: term and cash value. Term insurance lets you buy protection and only protection in case you die. In general, term insurance is a better buy. Cash value insurance is protection plus something else, usually a savings program. You get less protection for your dollar, plus a lower rate of return. There are four main types of cash value life insurance: whole life, universal life, variable life, and single premium. Spend as little on life insurance as possible.

4. Credit life is an expensive type of term insurance that gives you no control over its value. This is the type of insurance you are offered when you take out a car loan. Avoid it.

5. Consider the tax consequences of your life insurance policies; they do not go through probate but are taxable for federal estate tax purposes. State estate laws differ.

**6.** Everyone needs disability insurance because in middle age, you're more likely to become disabled than die. Don't assume that your company disability insurance will take care of you. Most company policies don't have enough coverage or have too many restrictions.

**7.** To evaluate companies and policies, check existing reports and use the ABC approach.

# CHAPTER 7

# Liabilities

**A** liability is anything that you owe to someone else: money, property, or services. A debt is money that you owe to someone else. Rent is not considered a debt, assuming you paid it on time.

By now, you should have completed the worksheets in Chapter 2, so you can refer back to them for a list of your liabilities. If you haven't yet pulled out your financial records or filled out the worksheets, please stop now and do so. Without the basic facts, you cannot reach your financial goals.

## Good Reasons to Borrow Money

There are three good reasons to borrow money:

**1.** You have a genuine emergency. For example, the furnace stops working in the middle of winter, the roof gets damaged in a storm and needs immediate repairs, or a medical emergency occurs. These are all justifiable reasons for borrowing money. Make sure it is a real emergency and not just an excuse to increase your spending.

**2.** You need to establish a credit history. Everyone needs a credit history so that, if an emergency occurs, you will be able to get a loan. Everyone also needs a personal credit history. If you're married and all the credit is in one spouse's name, it will be much more difficult to establish a personal credit rating if the credit holder dies, is disabled, or the couple divorces.

**3.** You borrow from yourself and pay yourself interest. Let's say you have money in an investment that's paying 9 percent; a car loan will cost 11 percent. It makes sense to use the investment money to buy the car. Then you pay yourself back with the monthly payments that you would otherwise have made to someone else.

## Bad Reasons to Borrow

Unfortunately, most of us borrow for bad reasons. Here are seven:

1. You borrow money to buy an experience. Unfortunately, you will still be paying off the loan when that great mountain scenery or week of Broadway plays is only a memory.

2. You borrow to buy something that depreciates: a car, a refrigerator, or a TV. You keep paying on the original cost while the value goes down and down. If you had an emergency and needed to pay off the loan, money received from selling the item would not cover the remainder of the loan.

3. You cannot afford to pay cash. In case you've forgotten this crucial concept from the Introduction, let me repeat myself: do not spend more than you earn. With very few exceptions (such as a genuine emergency), if you do not have the cash to buy something today, you should not borrow to buy it.

4. You are buying on impulse. If you see a bargain and really need the item, that's fine. Don't go out and buy something because you're feeling blue. There's nothing wrong with rewarding yourself occasionally, but if you get in the habit of shopping for an emotional lift, you will have a debt problem. No matter how good a deal you get, don't go into debt to buy something you really don't need.

5. You borrow to keep up with the Joneses (or the Rockefellers). Your neighbors may appear to be living the good life and yet be deeply in debt. That obstacle—ego—can keep you from achieving financial independence. Set your priorities and stick to them.

6. You expect to get a raise, bonus, and so on. Never base financial plans on what might happen. Until you see the money in your paycheck, do not spend it.

7. You are going to speculate with the money. Borrow to buy stock when the market is going up and you can easily lose that stock and still owe the original loan amount.

If you are borrowing for any of these seven reasons, you have a problem with your liabilities, whether or not you want to admit it.

# Types of Credit

Let's look at the types of credit available. They break down into four types: consumer, mortgage, home equity, and business.

## Consumer

This is the credit that most of us have used at one time or another. When you buy a car and finance it, take out a personal loan to fix up the house, or charge a new TV on your credit card, you are using consumer credit. Let's look briefly at car loans and credit cards.

## Car Loans

Have you noticed that most car ads no longer say how much the car costs—that would be too much of a shock—but how much the monthly payments are? As car costs have escalated, the monthly payments on a two-year loan have become more than the average person can handle. So the banks and other lenders have begun offering four- and five-year car loans. Now your car can rust out from under you while you're still paying for it.

Most of us take out our first car loans when we start our first jobs. Then we borrow again when we need a new car to replace the old one. We never get out from under that car debt. Start saving for your next car. Pay cash and save all that interest you used to pay.

Instead of buying a car, some people lease a car. A lease is an agreement to rent a car for a certain number of months or years. Table 7.1 summarizes the differences between leasing and buying a car, as outlined in the Federal Reserve Board's free consumer publication, *Keys to Vehicle Leasing*.

For more information on the decision to buy or to lease, you can get the entire Federal Reserve Board's booklet on leasing at www.bog .frb.fed.uspubsleasing). Kiplinger's *Personal Finance* magazine usually has an article about leasing every year and has an online calculator to help in

**TABLE 7.1**

# Should I Lease or Buy a Car?

| Considerations | Leasing | Buying |
|---|---|---|
| Ownership | You do not own the vehicle. | You own the vehicle. |
| Up-front cost | May include first month's payment, refundable deposit, a down payment, taxes, registration, and other fees. | Cash price or a down payment, taxes, registration, and other fees. |
| Monthly payments | Payments may be lower than a loan payment. | Payments are higher because you pay for everything up front. |
| Early termination | If you end the lease early, you may pay early termination charges. | If you have a loan and pay it off early, you owe the payoff amount. |
| Vehicle return | You may return the vehicle at lease end and pay any end-of-lease costs. | You can sell or trade the vehicle. |
| Future value | Whoever leased the vehicle to you has the risk of the future market value. | You have the risk of the vehicle's market value when you trade or sell it. |
| Mileage | Number of miles you can drive without added costs is limited, though you can negotiate a higher limit. | Drive all you want; higher mileage lowers trade-in value. |
| Excess wear | Possible excess wear charges. | No charges, but excess wear lowers trade-in value. |
| End of term | At the end of the lease, you may have a new payment for this or another vehicle. | At the end of the loan, no other payments. |

*Source:* Federal Reserve Board, *Keys to Vehicle Leasing.*

the lease–buy decision (www.kiplinger.com/calc). The Better Business Bureau also has leasing info at www.bbb.orglibraryautolease.html.

## Credit Cards

Credit cards come in two types: charge cards, which allow you to pay off purchases over time and charge an annual interest rate, and travel and entertainment cards, which require that you pay the entire bill every month. One of each should be enough for you. As long as you pay off the balance each month, these cards can be very useful. They supply a detailed list of expenditures for business or personal recordkeeping, and they are invaluable in a genuine emergency.

The main problem with credit cards of either type comes when people don't handle them responsibly. Do you pay the full balance every month? Or do you pay the minimum possible amount? If you regularly pay finance charges, if you typically run a balance, if you have more than a few cards, and especially if you use one card to pay off another, you have a credit problem. Take a look at the debt ratios discussed later in this chapter.

## Mortgage

This is the largest loan most people will ever have. Despite the different names a banker may give, there are only two types of mortgages: fixed and variable. Because choosing a mortgage depends so much on individual factors and the market, I can't tell you which one is right for you. Consult with your financial planner and read up-to-date books and articles to help you decide.

Before you even begin to look at houses, read Chapter 5. A home may not be the investment you thought it was. The points made in that chapter will give you a new perspective on home ownership.

## Home Equity Loans

Are home equity loans deductible? Yes, but that doesn't mean you should have one. Go back and reread the good and bad reasons to borrow. These reasons are especially true when it comes to a home equity loan. The interest is deductible, though how much you can deduct depends on the home's basis and its current value. Before you consider a home equity loan, talk it over with your financial planner and other advisors to be sure you understand the likely tax consequences.

## Business

If you have a second business (I believe everyone can benefit from a sideline business), you may need a business loan. If you're just starting out, you'll need a good business plan to show that you know what you're doing. If you're already in business, you'll need a current profit-and-loss statement, as well as other details about your business. Don't let the terms *business plan* and *profit and loss* scare you if they are unfamiliar. Check with your local Small Business Administration office for information and assistance. Use your library as an information resource. There are many books on starting a second business and creating a business plan. An accountant can help you prepare a profit-and-loss statement.

## Get the Best Loan

Whether you need a business or personal loan, there are four ways to get the money:

1. Through an installment loan (the worst kind), which will cost you the most interest. You pay almost all interest in the beginning of the loan, switching to principal at the end.

2. Through an interest and principal loan, in which you pay off the principal in approximately equal amounts each time you pay.

3. Through an interest-only loan, in which you pay only the interest due, not the principal. If you already have large amounts in certificates of deposit or other investments at a bank, you can try to get an interest-only loan from them. A loan on the cash value of your life insurance may be an interest-only loan. See Chapter 6 for cautions about loans against your insurance.

4. Through yourself (the best kind of loan). Borrow from savings. Pay yourself back each month.

If you must get a loan, shop around for the best rate and terms. Try to get a simple (not compound) interest loan. If you can pay it off early, you won't be penalized. Avoid loans that assess a penalty if you prepay the loan.

## How Much Debt Is Too Much?

Check yourself on the following four debt ratios:

**1.** Percent of debt to income. Look at your balance sheet to determine this ratio.

**2.** Total debt payments should total no more than 36 percent of your gross income.

**3.** Consumer debt should be no more than 20 percent of your gross income.

**4.** The ratio of take-home pay to debt service charges (the interest you pay to have a loan) should go down over time, not up.

## Establishing Credit

Unsolicited credit card applications hit mailboxes all over America every day. However, if you are just out of school or recently divorced or widowed, you may not have a credit history.

To establish credit, you can use a prepaid credit card, or collateral, usually a savings account. You take out a loan against the collateral. Then you pay off the loan before it is due, establishing that you can responsibly handle debt. Most loans require a demonstration that you have the income, the stability, and the responsibility to pay off the loan. You may have to take out several increasingly larger loans in order to get to your credit goal. Don't be afraid to ask the credit officer for a higher credit line.

A word to the wise married couple: establish your credit history in both names before you need it. Any of the many family finance books on the market have detailed discussions of how to establish credit.

## How to Get Out of Debt

What happens if you are so badly in debt that you think you can never get out? Or if you're just beginning to exceed acceptable debt ratios? Unfortunately, a complete discussion of this subject is beyond this book. Books such as *The Credit Repair Kit* or *All about Credit* discuss this topic.

However, I recommend these three steps.

1. Make it a priority to get out of debt. Commit to it. This is the hardest part psychologically.

2. Cancel your credit cards.

3. Go to a free credit-counseling service such as the Consumer Credit Counseling Service, which has branches all over the United States. Most large cities have one. Professionals there know how to help you get yourself out of debt. They will help you deal with your creditors and set up a realistic repayment schedule. It will not be painless, but you must do it.

Beware of companies that say they can get you out of debt and charge you for the privilege. The fact that they have to advertise tells you something. You could end up both in debt and out whatever money you pay them.

## Conclusion

Don't kid yourself about your liabilities. You *must* complete the worksheets in Chapter 2, so you will know where you stand. I'm not saying you should never have any debt. With proper financial planning, you can manage your liabilities. Be honest with yourself and take action when it's needed.

## Summary

1. A liability is anything you owe to someone else: money, property, or services. The worksheets you completed in Chapter 2 will give you a list of your liabilities.

2. Most Americans save little of their income while running up consumer debt. You must live on what you earn.

3. Establish your credit before you really need it.

4. How do you get out of debt when you're in over your head? First, commit yourself to the goal of getting out of debt. Second, cut up your credit cards. Third, go to a free credit-counseling service and let it help you. It won't be painless, but you can do it.

# CHAPTER 8

# Taxes

Reducing your income taxes is another way to meet your financial goals faster, by giving you more money to invest or spend. In this chapter, you will learn four different methods of tax reduction and specific tools to use. You must evaluate your situation to see if a particular strategy fits your total financial plan. Don't be an aggressive taxpayer. Pay what you owe but no more.

Before we move forward, however, I want to point out the single biggest mistake that taxpayers make. If you receive a large refund on your federal income tax, that's not a bonus. It's money that you loaned to the government, without charging interest. If you're paying too much in withholding tax, no matter what month it is, you still may be able to adjust the withholding on this year's taxes. Ask your financial professional to calculate what your withholding should be so that you're within a few hundred dollars of what you owe. Likewise, if some unexpected financial event has occurred (a bonus, a new baby, loss of a job, etc.), you may want to adjust your withholding tax up or down accordingly.

Meet with your accountant in the fall, or do a dry run on TurboTax or another online tool to get a sense of where you stand. You want to avoid tax surprises when you fill out the forms in January. If you don't use an accountant, the library has several tax planning books that will cover tax planning in the fall. Be sure to get the current year's book.

## Four Methods for Reducing Taxes

There are four methods for reducing taxes:

1. Splitting
2. Deferring
3. Converting
4. Sheltering

I'll cover the basics about how each method works and then look at specific examples in the section called "Tax Tools." Discuss each of these methods with your financial planner to see whether they fit your financial plan. Many of these tools have contribution limits that change over time. An online search will quickly tell you the current limits for whichever tools you consider.

## Splitting

The government would like to tax one big pile of your money. But you'll pay less if you split your income into smaller piles. You can split taxes by using family members, time, and tax tools (more on these later).

To split your income with family members, employ your children in a sideline business. Usually they will be taxed at a lower rate than the one you pay. Your 10-year-old can file papers or sweep floors or maybe run your spreadsheets or payroll. Discuss this strategy with your financial advisor to be sure you understand what work your children can do, how many hours they can work, and any other restrictions.

Of course, you'll need to consider how much money you want your children to have and so on. Reread Chapter 4 on education, which covers the issue of financial control.

To split your income by time, use an installment sale to postpone income to later years. To split income with a tax tool, you could use a non–service corporation to split income between yourself and the corporation.

Here's a very simple example of how splitting can reduce your taxes. Let's say you expect $100,000 in income. You receive it all in one year, during which your federal tax rate is 33 percent. (The tax rates are for illustration only, and I'm ignoring any other taxes, income, or deductions.) You would pay $20,381 in federal taxes.

Your income can be split between you and a family member— perhaps $60,000 to you and $40,000 to your child—and your tax rate would drop to 28 percent. You would pay federal taxes of $8,781. The child's tax rate, assuming she is older than 14, would be 28 percent, or $7,195 in taxes. The total federal tax bill? $15,976, for a savings of $ 4,405 in federal taxes.

Use a corporation in your split and your tax reduction can be even more dramatic. Don't forget that splitting is not assigning income. Check with your tax attorney or accountant on whether you can split income and how to do it correctly.

## Deferring

If you could choose between paying taxes today or paying taxes in 30 years, which would you choose? You could save money by deferring the tax with a tool, such as an IRA, A Simplified Employee Pension Plan (SEP), 401(k), or other tax-deferred investment plan, instead of paying it each year.

When you put money into a tool such as an IRA, you don't pay taxes on the interest earned until you withdraw the money. Let's say you invest $2,000 each year in an IRA. After earning an average of 8 percent annually for 30 years, you would have $264,817.05. You would pay interest on withdrawals at your retirement tax rate, which may be lower than your tax rate while you're still working.

Or you could choose a Roth IRA instead, which lets you invest after-tax dollars. The same investment of $2,000 each year for 30 years at an average of 8 percent annually would also total $264,817.05. But you would owe no taxes on your withdrawals. Whether it's better for you to pay taxes now or later is a matter for you and your planner to discuss. If you can afford to invest after-tax dollars, a Roth is often the better choice.

In addition to using a tool for deferral, you can defer taxes through a variety of financial products that offer deferral as part of their essential natures. These products include:

- Series EE bonds or other bonds
- Installment sales
- Certificates of deposit
- Treasury bills
- Treasury bills, notes, and bonds
- Corporate coupon bonds

## Series EE bonds and HH bonds

In the year you purchase these bonds, you can choose whether or not to declare earned interest for that year's federal income taxes. This establishes your intent to declare the interest every year. If you choose not to declare it for that year, you will pay taxes on the interest earned when you redeem the bonds, thus deferring the taxes.

This deferral has obvious advantages for parents who buy bonds for their children. Children under age 14 are taxed at their parents' rate after the first $1,200 of unearned income. Holding these bonds until the child is 14 will not only defer taxes, but also allow the interest to be taxed at the child's rate: a double benefit, allowing you to save more. Remember that when you give money to your children, it is their money to do with as they wish.

You can only acquire a Series HH bond by exchanging a Series EE bond (or the older Series E) bond. If you have a Series EE bond that is maturing and you do not want to cash it in, you may convert it into a Series HH bond, thus deferring the interest for an additional 20 years. You must declare the semiannual interest on a Series HH bond. Series I bonds are indexed for inflation.

## Annuities

The plain annuity ensures that a person who lives beyond her or his life expectancy won't run out of money. You pay no taxes on annuity earnings until you receive the money.

How does an annuity work? There are two basic ways to buy one:

**1.** For a plain annuity, you give the insurance company a very large amount of money at retirement and receive a monthly benefit.

**2.** You can pay an annuity premium annually, as with any other insurance policy, and collect a monthly benefit at retirement.

There are two ways to defer taxes through an annuity. A plain annuity's earnings are not currently taxable. When you pull the money out, you pay taxes on some of the money withdrawn, according to an IRS formula. You receive no tax deduction when you buy the annuity.

If you work for a public, nonprofit institution, such as a hospital, school, university, or charity, you can set up a tax-deferred, or 403(b) annuity. The amount you contribute reduces your salary, because you contribute to the annuity with pretax dollars. The initial contribution and its earnings are not taxable until you receive a distribution. There is a limit on how much you can put away each year.

There are four ways to distribute annuity benefits. Except for a refund, distributions can be fixed or variable amounts.

**1.** Straight life, which makes monthly payments for the rest of your life

**2.** Certain installments, which gives you monthly payments but also guarantees that you or your heirs will receive a stated minimum amount, no matter how long you live

**3.** Refund, in which you receive a lump sum refund of the amount in the annuity account

**4.** Joint and survivor, which gives you payments over your life and that of your survivor. This choice would give you lower payments but extend the payments over your spouse or another beneficiary's life.

Discuss the implications of these payment methods with your planner before you set up an annuity or sign any distribution agreement.

## Installment Sales

An installment sale of a business or other property can defer taxes for a short or long period. Even though the goal is to reduce taxes by deferring income, you'll need to consider other factors as well. Do you need the income today? Will your income be higher or lower in coming years? Are there other financial events that might affect this sale? Discuss this deferral strategy very carefully with your financial advisor.

## Certificates of Deposit

Certificates of deposit (CDs) can be used to defer taxes. You pay taxes on the interest a CD earns when the bank pays you that interest. Start the CD in December and you won't owe tax on the interest until sometime the next year.

### Treasury Bills
You pay federal taxes—no state or local taxes—when the bill matures.

### Treasury Notes and Bonds
Notes and bonds give you only a short deferral, because you get interest every six months. When the note or bond matures, it pays you back the principal. You owe no state or local taxes.

### Corporate Coupon Bonds
As with Treasury bonds, taxes are due on the interest earned when the coupon is paid on corporate coupon bonds.

## Converting

Converting changes income or expenses from one status to another. Here are three ways to convert:

**1.** Convert nondeductible to deductible.

**2.** Convert ordinary income to capital gain.

**3.** Convert through an equity transfer.

I'll briefly outline each technique. You must discuss converting techniques with your financial advisor to know whether they are appropriate for your situation.

### Convert Nondeductible to Deductible
As I've mentioned already, I believe everyone should have a second business for either extra income or tax benefits. A sideline business can help you convert nondeductible expenses such as travel, entertainment, and insurance to deductible expenses, saving on taxes and giving you more cash to spend or invest.

### Convert Ordinary Income to Capital Gain
Capital gains can also be a form of tax deferral. Taxes are not due until the capital gain is realized, so even if capital gains are taxed at the same rate as ordinary income, it still makes sense to convert

ordinary income to capital gain in order to defer taxes. Real estate is one possible route.

### Convert through an Equity Transfer

Let's say you work for a school and can contribute to a tax-deferred annuity. You expect to receive $15,000 from the sale of some real estate. You can do an equity transfer by increasing your tax-deferred annuity contribution to the maximum allowed and using the $15,000 for living expenses. This converts the $15,000 into a tax-deferred tool. Without doing this, you would have had to pay taxes on your pay and on your real estate profit, then take what's left and invest it. With an equity transfer, you can invest the full $15,000.

## Sheltering

A tax shelter is any investment that you invest in for the main purpose of changing ordinary income, which is taxable at a higher rate, into income that's taxed at a lower rate.

Too often, I see people chasing questionable and risky tax shelters when good financial planning can easily reduce their taxes with much lower risk. These people are tripped up by two of those obstacles I talked about in the Introduction: ego and lack of a plan. Without a good financial plan, you are easy prey for the hot tips that aren't really so hot. Remember, there are no great deals, just good planning.

One legitimate way to shelter income is through investment real estate. When it's in the downward part of its cycle, real estate is not a great investment. However, there are still ways to use real estate to shelter income from taxes, primarily depreciation. Real estate will be a better investment when the cycle turns back up.

## Tax Tools

A variety of tax-reducing tools are available to you, and you should investigate and use the tools that benefit you the most. The following list describes the most important candidates.

## Corporation

Although the tax rates have changed and will likely change again, there are still advantages to having a corporation. For example, the corporation can hold stock and reduce the tax paid on the dividends. Family members can be corporation shareholders and receive dividends, and they can be employees and participate in benefits such as a retirement plan, life insurance, and medical and dental coverage. Be sure to compare the price difference between buying these things personally to the cost of buying them as a corporation.

## Your Own Business

I believe you should have your own business. If you are an employee, you need a second business for the tax deductions. If you are making less than $50,000, you need a second business because you need the money. If you are making more than $50,000 per year, you need a second business because you need the tax deductions. As long as expenses are legitimately business related, a second business lets you convert nondeductible expenses into deductible expenses for:

- Trips
- Car and transportation
- Entertainment
- Fringe benefits (medical insurance, car insurance, etc.)
- Home office

A business also lets you shift highly taxed income to your children.

Business expenses are subtracted from business income and affect your adjusted gross income. Also, business expenses are not subject to the 2 percent threshold that applies to a miscellaneous itemized deduction.

## Keogh and IRA

If you have a business that is set up as a sole proprietorship or partnership, you can set up a Keogh retirement plan. It can be either a pension or profit-sharing plan and is subject to the same limitations as corporate plans. The tax law changes in 1986 and later years set the theoretical amount for defined-contribution plans at the lesser of 25 percent of net earnings from self-employment or $30,000, but it never quite equals that much because of the calculations. Profit-sharing plans let you deduct up to 15 percent of any employee's compensation. In either case, the amount contributed is tax deductible. You pay taxes on principal and interest when you withdraw it.

## IRA and Roth IRA

Everyone should have an IRA, unless they have already used other tools to save enough toward their goals. You can choose between the traditional IRA and the Roth IRA. Contributions to the traditional IRA are tax deductible, up to certain income limits. (Nondeductible IRAs are also an option for those who do not qualify for deductible IRAs.) When you take money out at retirement, you pay according to your current tax rate.

Contributions to a Roth IRA are not tax deductible when you set it up, but you pay no tax when you withdraw money at retirement. If you believe that your tax rate will be the same or higher when you retire, then the Roth IRA is probably for you. Consult a financial advisor to see what's best for your specific situation.

Even if the traditional IRA were not tax deductible, it's still a good tool, because the interest is tax deferred. There is a good chance that you will be in a lower tax bracket at retirement than when you are still working, so you'll pay less tax then than you would now.

## Simplified Employment Plans

A simplified employment plan (SEP) is similar to an IRA, except that your employer makes the contribution. SEP contributions are tax-deductible when you make them; you pay taxes at your current rate when you withdraw money at retirement.

## Savings Incentive Match Plan for Employees

The Savings Incentive Match Plan for Employees (SIMPLE) is a retirement plan designed for small businesses with 100 or fewer workers. Usually the employer matches up to 3 percent of employee contributions or contributes 2 percent of pay for each employee, even if the employee does not contribute. Self-employed business owners with no employees are allowed to contribute as well.

## Nonqualified Deferred Compensation Plans

These plans are an agreement between you and your employer. Your employer agrees to set aside money. If it's there when you retire, you get the money. If it's not, you don't. What can go wrong? The company may go out of business, get sued, or be sold. Deferred compensation plans are usually only available to executives, and are typically only part of a retirement plan.

## 403(b) Plans

These tax-deferred plans are available to those who work for public, nonprofit institutions, such as universities or public hospitals. You pay no tax on the contribution and usually have some options as to how your money is invested. There are provisions for making up contributions from years in which you were eligible but did not participate.

## Thrift and Savings Plans

Generally, these employer-based plans are not tax deferred. A thrift plan can include a 401(k), which is tax deferred, plus portions that are not tax deferred. Your employer may match your contribution.

## Voluntary Contributions

Although voluntary contributions are not tax deductible, the earnings are tax deferred. When you withdraw some of the money, the IRS considers the money part principal (not taxable) and part interest (taxable). Because there is no withdrawal penalty on the principal, the voluntary contribution is an excellent tool to use for an education fund. If your employer has already contributed the maximum amount to your retirement plan, then you may not make any voluntary contribution.

## Summary

1. We all should pay our fair share of taxes, but fairness is at least partially negotiable. By using these tax tools and tax-reduction methods, you can legally reduce your taxes.

2. You can increase your savings and achieve your goals sooner by reducing your income taxes. Evaluate any tax strategy as just one part of your financial plan.

3. Tools are techniques that help you reduce taxes. Possibilities include:

   - Pension and profit-sharing plans
   - 401(k) or CODA plans
   - Corporation
   - Your own business
   - Keogh
   - IRA and Roth IRA
   - Employee stock ownership plans (ESOP)
   - Simplified employment plans (SEP)
   - Nonqualified deferred compensation plans
   - 403(b) plans

- Thrift and savings plans
- Voluntary contributions

**4.** Most plans impose a penalty if you withdraw money before you reach age 59, except under some hardship circumstances.

**5.** Tax laws will continue to change. Let your financial advisors keep up on the details. Use the spendable cash worksheet to evaluate how a tool will help you.

# CHAPTER 9

# Investments

If this is the first chapter you're reading, stop. You've started at the wrong end of the book.

Financial planning is like painting a house. Strangely enough, the project's success really doesn't depend on the painting. Sure, it's helpful to pick a nice color and apply it evenly. But it's even more important to wash the walls first, spackle the holes and cracks, use a good primer and a clean brush, sand the surfaces smooth, employ drop cloths, and tape around anything you don't want to paint. The paint is the icing atop a cake that's made of preparations. Do those preparations well or the paint job won't look good.

Investing is a lot like that paint job. The concepts and work in the rest of the book are much more important than this chapter. They will make or break your financial plan. If you just read this chapter, you may do okay with your investments. But you won't have a financial plan. You'll go from investment to investment, as so many people do, but you may never reach financial independence. If it's important to you to be financially independent (and I can't imagine anyone not wanting that), please go back and read those chapters and do those worksheets. It's your money and your future; it's worth the time it will take. I've seen people turn their lives around once they finally developed a personal financial plan and stuck to it. You can do it, too.

In this chapter, I'll review the basics of saving and investing. You need to understand the foundation on which your investments will be based and how the financial cycles work. Then we'll look at risk and get into the details of a proven investment strategy that will let you beat inflation by 2 percent a year. I know that doesn't sound like much, but if you can do that, you should be able to meet your goals. I'll also cover investment mistakes to avoid and whether you should borrow to fund investments.

# Financial Basics

Before I talk about how to invest and what to invest in, let's review the basics. Here's the first basic fact: You have to have money to invest before you can invest. Where does it come from? It comes from your savings.

## Savings

Your savings, in turn, come from your earnings. Pay yourself first from every paycheck, and you will have money to invest. Don't wait for your ship to come in before you start saving; your boat may never get out of dry dock. Don't wait for an inheritance; don't wait to hit it big in the lottery. Don't wait! You must take the initiative and make the commitment to save money from every single paycheck. I know it will take discipline. For some people it's harder than for others, but you must save first.

## Understanding Compound Interest

Besides saving more, you need to be an informed saver. Do you know how often the interest is compounded on your current savings accounts? How often the interest is compounded and when it is paid make a big difference over the long run and may mean the difference between whether you can meet your goals.

Table 9.1 shows the difference among the compounding periods. Let's say you are saving $1,000 a year. Figure 9.1 shows you the comparison between annual, monthly, and daily compounding. Be sure to find out how quickly your interest compounds when shopping for a place to put your savings. Also ask when the interest is paid.

## Save in January

Always save at the beginning—not the end—of the year, so that you get the full benefit of a year of compound interest. Back in the Introduction, I mentioned that if you moved your funds from saving to spending one year too soon, you might not reach your goals. How can you figure

**TABLE 9.1**

# Difference among the Compounding Periods

The true interest rate varies depending upon the compounding period. If the stated rate of return is 5 percent, the real rate, based on how often dividends are paid, is as shown.

| | |
|---|---|
| Annually | 5.000% |
| Semi-annually | 5.063% |
| Quarterly | 5.094% |
| Monthly | 5.120% |
| Weekly | 5.125% |
| Continuously | 5.127% |

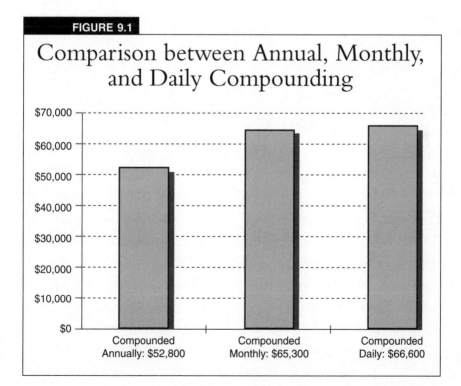

**FIGURE 9.1**

Comparison between Annual, Monthly, and Daily Compounding

**FIGURE 9.2**

# Basic Calculation

| Year | Amount Saved Each Year | Amount from Last Year | Amount to Invest for This Year | 10% Interest Rate + 1 | Value at End of Year |
|------|------------------------|-----------------------|--------------------------------|-----------------------|----------------------|
| 1 | $2,000 + | 0 = | $2,000 × | 1.10 = | $2,200 |
| 2 | $2,000 + | $2,200 = | $4,200 × | 1.10 = | $4,620 |
| and so on | | | | | |

out what a difference one year can make for you? Figure 9.2 shows the basic calculation, using savings of $2,000 per year, an interest rate of 10 percent, and reinvestment of interest. I realize your goal may be higher or lower than $2,000 each year, and the rate you earn may be different, but this concept is valid regardless of the amounts and rates.

Figure 9.3 shows the cost to wait one year at various times during the life of your investment. Notice that between year 1 and year 2, the difference between the cost of waiting for one year is $2,160 for an 8 percent return and $2,200 for a 10 percent return.

The cost of waiting grows even larger as the years pass. Look at the difference after 40 years: more than $40,000 at the 8 percent rate and more than $82,000 at the 10 percent rate! You can see how valuable that first dollar of savings can be.

## Avoid Leakage

I mentioned leakage in the Introduction as an obstacle to becoming wealthy. It's worth repeating here. You can't meet your goals if you spend the profits. When you get a bonus, save it. When you earn interest, reinvest it. I know that $100 will seem like a small amount at the time. But if you don't stick with your plan and discipline yourself to reinvest, you'll slip further and further behind.

**FIGURE 9.3**

# Cost to Wait One Year at Various Times during the Life of Your Investment

| Year | 8% Value at Start of Year | 8% Cost to Wait One Year | 10% Value at Start of Year | 10% Cost to Wait One Year |
|---|---|---|---|---|
| 1 | $ 2,000 | | $ 2,000 | |
| 2 | $ 4,160 | $ 2,160 | $ 4,200 | $ 2,200 |
| 3 | $ 6,493 | $ 2,333 | $ 6,620 | $ 2,420 |
| 4 | $ 9,012 | $ 2,519 | $ 9,282 | $ 2,662 |
| 5 | $ 10,733 | $ 2,721 | $ 12,210 | $ 2,928 |
| 9 | $ 24,975 | | $ 27,159 | |
| 10 | $ 28,973 | $ 3,998 | $ 31,875 | $ 4,716 |
| 14 | $ 48,430 | | $ 55,950 | |
| 15 | $ 54,304 | $ 5,874 | $ 63,545 | $ 7,595 |
| 17 | | | $ 81,089 | |
| 19 | $ 82,893 | | $102,318 | |
| 20 | $ 91,524 | $ 8,631 | $114,550 | $12,232 |
| 24 | $133,530 | | $176,995 | |
| 25 | $146,212 | $12,682 | $196,694 | $19,699 |
| 29 | $207,932 | | $297,262 | |
| 30 | $226,566 | $18,635 | $328,988 | $31,726 |
| 34 | $317,253 | | $490,953 | |
| 35 | $344,634 | $27,380 | $542,049 | $51,095 |
| 39 | $477,882 | | $802,896 | |
| 40 | $518,113 | $40,231 | $885,185 | $82,290 |

## How the Financial Cycle Works

Here's a basic definition of a financial cycle and how you can work with this cycle instead of against it. First, keep telling yourself that you can understand how to invest. You probably already know the basics of the financial cycle and don't realize it. Let's look at a simple example.

What if you could only put your money in money market funds or bonds? How would you decide which financial product to choose?

What happens when inflation goes up and interest rates go up? Businesses can't afford to borrow to finance growth. The stock market goes down. What to do? Use money market funds to keep up with rising rates.

What happens when interest rates go down? Businesses and individuals borrow and the stock market goes up. You want to lock in higher rates through long-term bonds as the rates begin to fall. Figure 9.4 summarizes the points of this simple example.

There are as many variations—stagflation, disinflation, and so on—as there are pages in the *Wall Street Journal*. I just want you to know what happens during the very basic up-and-down cycle. It won't

---

**FIGURE 9.4**

# How the Basic Financial Cycle Works

**Inflation goes up; interest rates rise**

- The stock market goes down
- Businesses can't afford to borrow
- Gold usually goes up
- Real estate may go up or down

**Your strategy?**

- Keep more money in cash equivalents (money market funds)

**Inflation goes down; interest rates go down**

- The stock market goes up
- Businesses and individuals borrow
- Gold usually goes down
- Real estate may go up or down

**Your strategy?**

- Use bonds to lock in falling interest rates for a longer term

work this way every time, of course, but you'll know what to watch for. A little later I'll show you how to use this knowledge to plan your investment strategy.

No matter where the financial cycle is on its roller-coaster ride, you should always have a diversified portfolio. Even if you are absolutely sure that you know what the cycle will do next, you should have a mix of stocks, bonds, and cash.

## Your Investment Goal

Your investment goal should always be to beat inflation by 2 percent per year after taxes and expenses, a number called the *real return*. I know a 2 percent return doesn't sound like much, but if you can do that, you'll be a winner. You may not make a 2 percent real return every year. Some years you'll do better, some years worse. However, over the years you should aim for about a 2 percent average real return. In all my years as a financial planner, I've seen that people reach their goal when they can beat inflation by just a modest amount.

When you prepare a good financial plan, you can take less risk and still meet your goal. This is good news. It means you don't have to dabble in pork bellies or exotic investments. Remember: the game is not how much you make, but whether you reach your goal.

To review, you save from your earnings. From those savings, you have money to invest. However, maybe the word *investing* sounds risky to you. Let's define *risk* and talk about how you can deal with it.

## Evaluating Risk

Even if you don't think you are investing, you are facing financial risk. The type of risk that everyone faces is inflation risk.

### Inflation Risk

Even if you never buy a stock or bond, you must deal with inflation risk. If you have your savings in a savings account yielding 4 percent and inflation is 3 percent, your real return is only 1 percent. Inflation can make your money lose some of its purchasing power over time. Over time, continuing inflation can compound into a very large loss of value. Inflation is your greatest enemy. Always has been, always will be—even at low rates.

## Other Types of Risk

Other types of financial risk include:

- **Principal or market risk**. You can lose money if you sell an investment for a price that's less than what you paid.

- **Interest rate risk**. Fixed-income securities that pay a specified interest rate lose some of their value if market interest rates rise.

- **Reinvestment rate risk**. Fixed-income securities have a specific maturity date. If you plan to buy another bond, you may or may not be able to purchase one at a favorable rate or yield.

- **Credit risk (default risk)**. A bond issuer could fail to pay the principal or interest when due. This is referred to as *default*. To compensate investors for the increased risk, issuers with poorer credit ratings generally pay a higher interest rate than do more stable borrowers.

There is always risk in investing. You just have to decide which risk you want to take. In addition, if you don't plan well, by the time you pay taxes on your investment earnings, you may have no return because the taxes have eroded your return.

How do you determine your risk level? Figure 9.5 is a risk evaluation checklist to understand your risk tolerance. Be honest with yourself as you answer these 10 questions.

Although the final rating you calculate may help you compare different investments, this table is really meant as a caution. I want you to think through a potential investment's risks and consider your real risk tolerance. If you are married, it is very helpful to see how you and your spouse answer these questions separately, so you can discuss possible differences in your risk tolerance.

**FIGURE 9.5**

# Risk Evaluation Checklist

| | Rate "5" | Rate "4" | Rate "3" | Rate "2" | Rate "I" | Score |
|---|---|---|---|---|---|---|
| What is the expected annual rate of return? | 14% | 12% | 10% | 8% | 6% | _____ |
| How liquid is the investment? | Immediate | 6mos. | 1 yr. | 2 yrs. | 20 yrs. | _____ |
| How much management time is required of you? | None | 25% | 50% | 75% | 100% | _____ |
| How long for the investment to mature? | Immediate | 6mos. | I yr. | 5yrs. | 10 yrs. or more | _____ |
| How inflation-proof is it? | Excellent | Good | Some | Almost None | None | _____ |
| What tax advantages are there? | Excellent | Good | Some | Almost None | None | _____ |
| How safe is your money? | Excellent | Good | Some | Almost None | None | _____ |
| Is there low interest rate fluctuation? | Excellent | Good | Some | Almost None | None | _____ |
| Can you tolerate this investment? (personal temperament) | Excellent | Good | Some | Almost None | None | _____ |
| What is the potential for the income promised? | Excellent | Good | Some | Almost None | None | _____ |
| Final Rating | | | | TOTAL | | _____ |

5 = Excellent
4 = Good
3 = Average
2 = Below average
I = Poor

Divide by 10 =
Final rating _____

## Investment Triangle

I developed the investment triangle in Figure 9.6 to help my clients choose investments based on the level of risk their situations would allow. You can use it to help plan your investment strategy and to keep your risk down. You should be able to beat inflation by 2 percent per year after taxes.

How does the investment triangle work? You invest only as much as your level of risk will allow. Using this method, the less money you have to invest, the more conservative you must be. For example, if you have only $10,000 to invest, you might put $3,500 in the defensive level, $3,000 in the conservative level, $2,000 in the moderate level, $1,000 in the aggressive level and $500 in the speculative level. What can you get for $500? Nothing, so you are forced back one level. Now you have $1,500 ($1,000 + $500) to put in the aggressive level. Or you can back off one more level and have $3,500 to invest at the moderate level. Either way, the amount you have to invest forces you to stay away from speculating. The exact percentages matter much less than the overall concepts that the triangle encapsulates:

**1.** Have an investment plan and stick with it.

**2.** Diversify, but don't spread yourself too thin.

**3.** Determine the level of risk you can afford.

The investment triangle approach takes these three concepts and combines them into a workable method. Don't make investing more complicated than it is. Always invest with a goal in mind and always ask yourself, "How does this investment fit my goal?" Make sure that your portfolio is structured to meet your goal, not to achieve open-ended performance.

Discuss your risk tolerance with your planner. If your planner suggests investments that you're not comfortable with, question the planner's reasons for recommending a particular investment. If the planner doesn't understand or accept your risk comfort level, find another advisor.

After you've determined your risk tolerance, you'll need a strategy to manage risk in your investments.

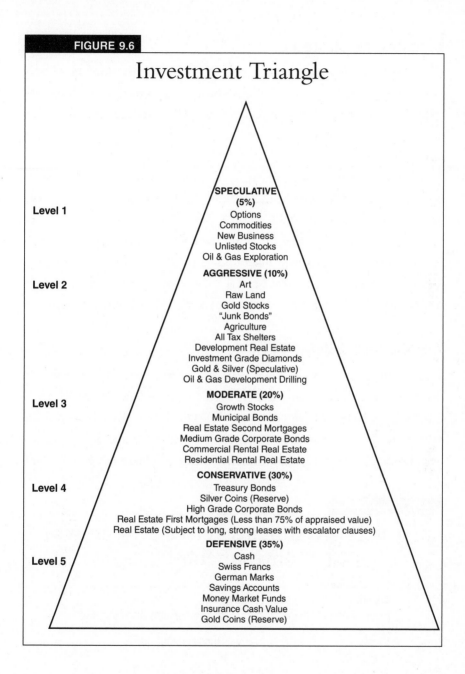

**FIGURE 9.6**

# Investment Triangle

**Level 1**

**SPECULATIVE**
**(5%)**
Options
Commodities
New Business
Unlisted Stocks
Oil & Gas Exploration

**Level 2**

**AGGRESSIVE (10%)**
Art
Raw Land
Gold Stocks
"Junk Bonds"
Agriculture
All Tax Shelters
Development Real Estate
Investment Grade Diamonds
Gold & Silver (Speculative)
Oil & Gas Development Drilling

**Level 3**

**MODERATE (20%)**
Growth Stocks
Municipal Bonds
Real Estate Second Mortgages
Medium Grade Corporate Bonds
Commercial Rental Real Estate
Residential Rental Real Estate

**Level 4**

**CONSERVATIVE (30%)**
Treasury Bonds
Silver Coins (Reserve)
High Grade Corporate Bonds
Real Estate First Mortgages (Less than 75% of appraised value)
Real Estate (Subject to long, strong leases with escalator clauses)

**Level 5**

**DEFENSIVE (35%)**
Cash
Swiss Francs
German Marks
Savings Accounts
Money Market Funds
Insurance Cash Value
Gold Coins (Reserve)

## Investment Strategy

Diversification helps you manage risk. To diversify, you don't buy just a little bit of everything. Some things you can't afford: fine art that costs millions of dollars, racehorses, homes in Venice, Italy. Some things do not provide consistent returns, robbing you of the value of compound interest.

The first step in diversification is to decide how much money you should have in growth investments and how much in nongrowth investments. (See Figure 9.7.)

Once you've determined how much you should put in growth and nongrowth investments, you need to decide what investments suit your needs. In growth, do stocks or real estate belong in your portfolio? In nongrowth, is a particular money market fund or bond a good fit?

### Your Decision Is Based on Time

The time between now and when you want to spend your investment decides how much of your portfolio should be in growth and nongrowth investments. How old are you? How long do you expect this portfolio to last—to the end of your life, right? So, if you are 45 and you expect to live until 85, there's a 40-year horizon. Of course, you're not going to put

---

**FIGURE 9.7**

# Growth Investments versus Nongrowth Investments

| Growth (appreciate over time) | Nongrowth (protect a certain amount of income) |
| --- | --- |
| Stocks | Money market mutual funds |
| Real estate | Bonds |
| Oil and gas | Savings accounts |
| Gold | CDs |
| | T-bills |
| | T-notes |

a dollar in today and leave it for 40 years without substantially changing your overall investment allocation to match your changing time horizon.

## Nongrowth Investments Protect You from Volatility

Here's another way to look at how much of your portfolio should be in growth and how much in nongrowth investments. The nongrowth portion is there to protect you from volatility. It's easy to see this principle in full-blown retirement. If you're fully retired, you take one year of cash flow and put it in money market funds. You take the next year's cash flow, plus inflation, and put it in a one-year T-bill. Then place year three, year four, and year five's cash flow, plus inflation, in three-, four-, and five-year T-bills, respectively. Now you have a five-year plan with your investments in a form called a ladder. You have five years to decide when to sell the funds.

You can use this approach even before retirement. How much nongrowth investments do you need, based on your safety needs? Do you want to have one year of income? Two years? Any answer can be correct; it depends on you and your specific situation.

## Asset Allocation Is Based on History

Prepare your financial plan, know the reasons a particular product will help you meet your goals, and then take action. Asset allocation is a concept which looks at how much you should have in growth and how much in nongrowth, based on past market history. Over a long time horizon, stocks have performed better than any other investment. If it's clear that you ought to be in the stock market, then you ought to be totally in the market (100 percent allocated), if you can stand the volatility. Even so, you'll need to protect yourself against volatility by having enough cash so that you don't have to worry about the market for some period of time. The amount of time depends on your horizon. A five- to seven-year nongrowth amount should be more than adequate, because market cycles tend to happen in that five- to seven-year period.

## How Much Do You Need in Reserve?

Don't forget that you need a cash reserve, as I discussed in Chapter 2, when you prepared your cash flow worksheet. Remember, a reserve is liquid cash you can get your hands on for emergencies, 24 hours a day. You need to have a reserve before you consider investing.

---

**TIP**

Your broker has a record. Check it! The Securities and Exchange Commission (www.sec.gov), the New York Stock Exchange (www .nyse.com), and the National Association of Securities Dealers (www .nasdr.com) can provide you with information.

---

## Timing the Market

A couple of words to those who think they can time the market: you can't. Several studies have shown that people often get out of the stock market in time, but they don't go back in time. They miss the best day for getting back, not getting out. That's why most people lose when they try to time the market. The number-one thing about successful investing is time. Stop trying to time the market. It's more important to be properly allocated. That goes back to growth, nongrowth, and the types of investments within those two areas.

## Nongrowth Investments

In the nongrowth area, I would probably stay away from CDs and bank accounts, because they often aren't as successful as other investments. By the time you get to an age at which your investment allocation should include bonds, you will likely have enough money to buy a bond that matures at your required date—a less-volatile strategy than buying a bond mutual fund. Remember that the bond price fluctuates. Nonetheless, I want to know that in one year, a specified number of dollars will free up that I can put into my money market fund or somewhere else where it's absolutely liquid. By laddering the maturity dates, I can plan a specific amount of income for each time period I choose.

## Growth Investments

Even though you can find a wealth of publicly available information, a mutual fund manager still knows more about the stock market than you do. Managers get first-hand information by visiting companies and getting to know executives. For a small investor, mutual funds are a terrific way to get started.

## Understanding the Investment Matrix

Review your investment strategy. First, you want some form of diversification: growth or nongrowth, based on your time horizon. Within growth, choose a type: mutual funds or stocks, for example. Within mutual funds, look at the investment style of the mutual fund you should buy.

Here's where the investment matrix is very helpful. The matrix looks like a small checkerboard with labels across the top squares and down one side. Stocks are ranked according to their investment style, and the appropriate box in the grid is shaded. The labels vary among investment-tracking firms. Morningstar uses "Large, Medium, Small" on the vertical side and "Value, Blend, and Growth" across the top, for a total of nine investment-style boxes. Value Line's grid has a rectangle of four boxes with four smaller boxes within each large one. Value Line's labels are "Large, Small" on the side and "Value, Growth" across the top. Both companies have sample reports on their websites, which show how they use their investment matrix (www.morningstar.com and www.valueline.com). Or you can find their reports at most libraries.

Depending on your age and how much time you have, you can look at the matrix and say, "If I'm 70 years old, the majority of my investments ought to be in the large-value box." Or "If I'm 21 years old, the majority of my investments ought to be in the small-growth box." As you get older, you move up from small to large, because there's less volatility in the large. By definition, there's less volatility in the value investment style than in the growth investment style.

As you build your portfolio, you may fill all of the boxes, but the percentages in the boxes will depend on where you are in your financial time horizon. You might have six large-value mutual funds and three small-growth mutual funds.

In general, I suggest that you stay away from balanced funds because they generally have a large number of bonds in them. That's not why we're buying them. We're looking for growth investments and bonds are nongrowth investments.

One reliable mutual funds indicator is the Sharpe ratio, listed in the Morningstar reports on each mutual fund. This ratio shows whether the return you're getting is worth the risk you're taking. The higher the number, the better, from the investor's point of view. A 1.0 is okay; the ratio goes up to about 3.

## Investment Choices

Now that you've learned about the financial cycle, risk, and diversifying to reduce risk, two of your choices should be obvious: bonds and cash. When I say cash, I mean money market funds, certificates of deposit, and even savings accounts, though, usually the first two pay more interest than does a savings account.

I also recommend mutual funds for your investment strategy. Let's look at bonds and mutual funds in more detail.

## Bonds

When you buy a bond, you loan money to the bond issuer. The issuer agrees to pay you a stated interest rate on that loan. This interest rate is also called the coupon rate. You receive the interest on a periodic basis. There are many variations on this basic premise. The advantage to you is the ability to lock in a fixed rate of return for a fixed time period.

If you intend to keep the bond until maturity, you don't necessarily need to worry about this next part. But if you want to trade your bond before maturity, then its market value is very important to you. You know the bond's rate of return, but its market value can still fluctuate with interest rates (and sometimes other factors). The difference between the bond's face value and its market value is called the yield, a number that typically moves in sync with market value. When interest rates go down, the value of higher-rate bonds goes up—and so does their yield. When rates go up, lower-rate bonds are less attractive, and so their yield falls.

When you are evaluating whether to buy bonds or to hold on to the ones you have, you must look at the rate of return, the bond's current value, and the income it produces for you, if any.

Figure 9.8 shows a simple example of how a bond's value can change. Notice that you still get the same income, but when interest rates go up, the bond's value drops to $500. This inverse relationship between rate and market value occurs because an investor can buy a new bond paying a higher rate of return. To get the same yield from your bond, a purchaser would need to pay you less.

When interest rates go down, the bond's value goes up, because an investor can't get the same return by purchasing a new bond and so is willing to pay more for yours.

There are many types of bonds: Treasury, Series EE, Series HH, agency, municipal, corporate, and zero coupon.

---

**FIGURE 9.8**

# Bond Market Value?

|  | Rate Now | Rate Goes Up | Rate Goes Down |
|---|---|---|---|
| Market rate | 10% | 20% | 5% |
| Value | $1,000 | $500 | $2,000 |
| Income per year | $100 | $100 | $100 |
| Interest | 10% | 20% | 5% |
| Divide income by market rate | | | |

## Treasury Bills

The U.S. government sells T-bills, which are similar to EE savings bonds. T-bills are sold in amounts of $10,000 or more for periods of 13 weeks, 26 weeks, or 52 weeks. You pay federal tax, but no state or local taxes on the interest. They can be purchased through any Federal Reserve Bank by mail or online. The general information website is www.freservices.org/treasury/frsreasury.cfm. For details on purchasing directly from the Federal Reserve Bank (called Treasury Direct), use www.publicdebt.treas.gov/sec/sectrilir.htm. If you are an existing Treasury Direct customer, use www.publicdebt.tres.gov/sec/secinnsr .htm. Check with your local library or bank for the address of the nearest Federal Reserve Bank. You can also purchase T-bills through other financial institutions, but you will pay them a fee to do so.

## Treasury Bonds and Notes

Treasury bonds (T-bonds) are also considered safe, because the U.S. government backs them. Sold for lower minimum amounts than T-bills, T-bonds are offered for longer periods of time.

Treasury notes (T-notes) have maturities of 1 to 10 years; T-bonds have maturities of 1 to 30 years. You receive interest payments every six months and owe no state or local taxes on that money. You get the principal back when the note or bond matures. You can buy Treasury bonds and notes through any Federal Reserve Bank by mail or using the web addresses listed in the section on T-bills.

## Agency Bonds

The government does not back agency bonds, but they are reasonably safe. Examples include:

1. Federal National Mortgage Association (FNMA or Fannie Mae) (www.fanniemae.com)

2. Government National Mortgage Association (GNMA or Ginnie Mae) (www.ginniemae.gov)

**3.** Federal Home Loan Mortgage Association (FHLMA or Freddie Mac) (www.freddiemac.com)

**4.** Student Loan Marketing Association (SLMA or Sallie Mae) (www .salliemae.com)

## Municipal Bonds

State governments, local governments, and local development districts (for example, water and sewer districts) can issue municipal bonds to fund their projects. Unless you happen to live in the area, you won't know much about the project. You'll need to do some research at your library. Two rating services—Moody's (www.moodys.com) and Standard and Poor's (www.standardandpoor.com)—evaluate the quality of these bonds and publicly publish the results.

## Corporate Bonds

Corporations issue bonds to raise money. Before you buy a corporate bond, check out the company using the ratings given by Moody's or Standard & Poor's.

## Corporate or Government Zero Coupon Bonds or STRIPS

This is a bond that's stripped of interest. The return is based on the difference between the price at issuance and the price at maturity. You pay taxes on the interest each year, even though you do not receive the interest until the bond matures.

## Mutual Funds

A mutual fund is a professionally managed corporation that invests in individual investments, such as stocks and bonds. There are many advantages to buying a mutual fund rather than the individual stocks.

- Professional management. Instead of spending your time reading and researching the stock market, you benefit (hopefully) from the knowledge and experience of professional managers and research staff.

- Diversification. You can own more stocks at a lower cost because the fund buys in volume and gets better transaction costs than you could for the amount you have invested. Most mutual funds require a small minimum investment and an even smaller minimum investment to invest through an IRA, so you can diversify even within your first IRA.

- Liquidity. Most funds are easily bought and sold on the open market. You can usually make portfolio changes within a day by making a phone call or going online.

- Flexibility. If you own shares in a fund that belongs to a family of funds, you can move back and forth more freely between funds with different styles. There is usually no fee.

## Mutual Fund Types

There are three types of mutual funds. I list some examples, so you can look them up in Value Line or Morningstar, but these are not recommendations.

1. Open-end investment companies. You buy shares from the fund and sell them back to the fund. Some examples include Vanguard 500 Index and Fidelity Magellan.

2. Closed-end investment companies. These companies have a fixed number of shares. No new shares are issued. Some examples include Gabelli Equity and Black Rock Income.

3. Investment trusts. You purchase an interest in an unmanaged investment pool. The trust agreement specifies the way in which the investments are held for safekeeping. Investors buy into the fund and hold that investment until the trust matures, or they sell their investment like a stock. One type of investment trust is a real estate investment trust (REIT).

## Charges

Some mutual funds levy a sales charge when you buy fund shares. This is called a front-end load. There may be other fees as well, such as a fee when you sell shares, called a back-end load, or exit fee. Funds that charge fees are called load funds. No-load funds do not have an initial sales charge but may charge you when you sell your shares.

## Evaluating Funds

Before you buy a mutual fund, evaluate a fund on the following three points:

1. Objectives. Read the prospectus. In the first few pages, you will find a description of the fund's objectives, which might include:

   - Aggressive growth
   - Growth
   - Growth and income
   - Income
   - Balanced
   - Index
   - International
   - Bond
   - Money market

   In addition, some funds specialize in certain market sectors, such as utilities or technology.

2. Performance. Perhaps the next most important consideration is performance. Who manages the fund? What's that person's tenure and track record? The yield mentioned in the prospectus can be calculated on as little as five days' results. Several mutual fund tracking reports show various funds' 1-, 5-, and 10-year performance. Morningstar (www.morningstar.com) and Value

Line (www.valueline.com) offer two of these reports. In addition, most business magazines have monthly columns or annual reports on mutual fund performance. Once again, do your research before you pick a fund.

3. Cost. The fund's selling price is called the net asset value, or NAV. It's the sum of all the fund's shares at market closing, divided by the number of mutual fund shares outstanding. The *buy* price is also called the public offering price, or POP. This is the investor's cost to buy one share of a mutual fund.

   Funds can charge you a variety of front- and back-end loads, annual sales charges, fees, and so on, and they're not always clearly described in the fund prospectus. Avoid funds with a 12b-1 charge, which covers the fund's selling and marketing costs. This fee can run up to 1.25 percent of your portfolio.

   The Securities and Exchange Commission requires that a fund prospectus show specific information on all charges, including 12b-1 charges.

   For more information on mutual funds, check our website (www.sestina.com) or the annual mutual fund issue of *Kiplinger's Personal Finance* (www.kiplinger.com).

4. Active versus passive management. Actively managed mutual funds try to achieve the best possible performance. Passively managed funds, also known as index funds, simply try to match their performance to one of many market indices. If the S&P 500 gains 5 percent this year, an index fund linked to the S&P 500 will endeavor to also gain 5 percent—no more, no less.

## Money Market Funds

A money market fund is a mutual fund that invests only in the money market: government securities, commercial paper, and negotiable certificates of deposit. If you are conservative and have a very low risk tolerance, consider money market funds that invest only in U.S. government bills and bonds. Remember: the lower the risk, the lower your rate of return. Although you may feel secure investing in a money market fund that has a lower risk, are you accumulating enough dollars to meet your investment goals?

## Evaluating Investments

How do you learn about investments and how to evaluate them? In Chapter 6, I explained the ABC approach to becoming an informed consumer on life insurance. Ask A, ask B, ask C. A looks at B, B looks at C, C at A. This approach will also work to look at stocks, bonds, mutual funds, or any investment.

Keep asking questions until you understand. Don't let the *trust me* attitude of some investment advisors bother you. It's your money they want to manage. If they're uncomfortable answering a lot of questions, go elsewhere.

## What Is My Rate of Return?

Rate of return is a major part of the sales pitch for any investment. You should consider each potential investment's true rate of return, not what the salesperson says you will get. No one investment does well all the time, so your investment plan needs diversification.

Never be out of an investment you eventually want to be in. Your crystal ball on what's ahead in the business cycle just might be wrong. As I tell my seminar attendees, those who live by the crystal ball must learn to eat ground glass.

## Measuring and Defining Returns

When you invest, you need to measure and define your return. Here are five measures of how your investment is doing.

1. What cash flow does the investment generate? Do you need income? If so, what cash flow range is acceptable?

2. Is your investment appreciating? What balance do you want between income and appreciation?

**3.** Are you building up any equity?

**4.** Does the investment have advantages for your tax situation?

**5.** Consider the interaction between investments. Can one investment offset the taxable gains of another?

# Common Investment Mistakes
## Excess Funds

Don't commit all your excess funds. Check your cash flow worksheet. (Go back and complete yours now if you haven't already done so.) If you consistently have a substantial surplus in your savings account every single month, go ahead and invest it. But be sure you're not investing your cash reserve. How much do you need for your emergency fund? Financial folklore says six months' pay. Don't rely on that. Figure out what's right for you with the help of your cash flow worksheet. You don't want to put all your excess funds in six-month T-bills and find out two months later that you need the money.

## Avarice

Do you try to wring the last penny out of a winning investment? Don't be tight-fisted and hold on to an investment for fear you'll lose a dime, especially when you've already made a dollar. Once you've doubled your money, you should sell half. If you have a plan, you decide before you make an investment when you should sell, instead of letting greed determine your actions. Another part of greed is letting the tax tail wag the economic dog. Don't buy an investment for tax reasons; buy it because it fits into your plan. Do the numbers. Is there any potential in the investment?

## Gluttony

Financial gluttons are excessive with their investments. Their eyes are always bigger than their purses. Gluttons get impatient, so they trade too much. They think they will generate a higher return, but all they generate is more commission for their brokers. They lack the discipline to make a plan and stick to it. Don't be distracted by the hope of making more.

## Gullibility

Don't believe everything you hear about an investment; don't buy on hunches, tips, and rumors. Any hot tip you hear is just a rumor. Insider trading is illegal. The people who are insiders can't and shouldn't tell you what to buy. Anyone else is just guessing. Buy based on facts.

## Sloth

Are you a lazy investor? Investing requires work. Some people spend more time researching and buying a car than they do learning about a potential investment. Do your homework. Find out everything you can before you put your money down. The most important factors are the people and their experiences. I'd rather be in a bad deal with good people than a good deal with bad people. Research individual managers at Morningstar, Kiplinger's, Yahoo Finance, or other online resources.

Supervise your investments once you've made them. It is so easy to let someone else do things for you. Don't turn your financial affairs, investments or otherwise, over to someone else. At the very least, you need to keep in touch so that you know what is happening and your designated advisor knows that you are a concerned investor. No one cares more about your money than you do.

## Pride

Don't let pride get in the way of your plan. When you make a mistake, admit it and move on. Stubborn pride makes you ride a loser all the way down. When an investment no longer fits your plan, get rid of the investment. Too many people worry about whether they made a good or bad decision or whether they sold too soon or too late. No financial plan is perfect.

## Cowardice

Sometimes it's not pride, but the fear of failure that trips you up. Remember that in financial planning, as in life, there is risk in everything you do. Driving a car is risky, but defensive driving techniques can lower the risk. Even eating seems risky these days, with our increased knowledge of the effects of different foods on our health. But you keep on driving and eating because you need to do them. You need a financial plan, too. If you do nothing, you face the risk that inflation will eat away at your purchasing power, that someone else will make the wrong decisions for you about your money, that changes in tax laws will take even more from your pocket.

## Conformity

Don't follow the herd. When an investment is recommended in the media, wait a week or two until the price settles down. The institutions buy before the little guy has a chance to buy, then the institutions sell after the little guy buys in. You lose! Buy an investment only if it fits your plan, not because everyone else is doing it.

## Overdiversification

It makes sense to diversify your investments. If one part of your investment portfolio suffers a loss, the overall portfolio is healthier when the other parts have not. The problem is that some people interpret this advice to mean that if a little bit of diversification is good, more is better. Don't own a little gold mining stock, a little real estate, some oil shares, a little in a money market fund, and a little in bonds. You'll be spread too thin and accomplish nothing.

## Underdiversification

There is no investment for all seasons. It would be easy if you could just park your money in one investment, come back in 30 years, and take your profits. Unfortunately, there are a few financial advisors who seem to believe this myth—or at least they want you to believe it and buy their advice. It just isn't true. The financial cycle causes fluctuations in all investments' value at one time or another, so diversification is important.

## Speculation

Here's that obstacle, ego, again. We all try to hit financial home runs. You can't afford the risk of speculation. Some advisors say that you should speculate while you're young. Look at that graph on the cost of losing one year of investing. Do you really want to blow that much money on an ego trip? Why speculate when you can meet your goals without it? Why postpone your financial freedom by even one year?

## Bargains

Don't buy because the investment looks like a bargain. Buy quality. An investment is only a bargain if it's something you would otherwise have purchased at a higher price.

## Fads

Don't buy fad investments. There will always be fads; leave them to someone else. They don't usually last long enough to be worth your time or money. Buy known financial products that will be here today and tomorrow.

## Experts

Don't assume that an expert in one thing is an expert in another. We're taught to respect authority. When you find someone who really is an expert in widgets, it's only human nature to ask for his or her opinion on thingamajigs. These experts are flattered or egotistical, so they tell you what they think. Just because they have an opinion doesn't mean they know what they're talking about.

## Borrowing to Fund Investments

Should you borrow to fund your investments? Answer three basic questions before you consider this strategy:

**1.** Will you pay yourself back? Do you have the discipline to do it? If not, don't borrow.

**2.** Look at your cash flow. Can you afford to pay the interest?

**3.** Look at your liabilities. Check those debt/income ratios that I mentioned in Chapter 7.

If you answer no to any of these questions, then this strategy is not for you. But if you meet these three tests, read on.

Remember to always contribute at the beginning of the year. What if you don't have the money? Consider borrowing it. Figure 9.9 shows how you can come out ahead. Let's say you borrow $2,000 at the beginning of the year and put it into an IRA earning 10 percent. Even with an interest rate of 12 percent on an installment loan, you would still be ahead. The difference between starting your IRA on January 2, even with a loan, and waiting until you have the money at the end of the year is $9,822 in this example.

---

**FIGURE 9.9**

## It Pays to Borrow for an IRA

| | |
|---|---:|
| Loan amount each year | $2,000 |
| Loan rate | 12% |
| Term (one-year loan every year for 30 years) | 1 year |
| Loan monthly payment | $177.67 |
| Interest paid for one-year loan | $132 |
| After-tax cost | $132 |
| Total paid for one-year loan | $2,132 |
| IRA earns | 10% |
| Cost to wait one year (value of $2,000 in 30 years) | $31,726 |
| Cost of interest paid for one year (the $132 could have grown to this amount) | $2,320 |
| Benefit to borrow so you can invest at beginning of the year | $29,406 |

Even with nondeductible interest, it still may be better to borrow. Let's say your goal is to save $25,000 each year. If you could earn 10 percent interest on your savings through investments, it would cost you $411,235 to wait one year. If you could borrow the money at 12 percent at the beginning of each year and pay it back in one year, the cost to borrow every year for 30 years would be $272,238. Your benefit to borrow ends up being $138,997.

Don't worry about these specific numbers. Your goal for annual savings may be more or less. I want you to understand why it might be better to borrow. You'll have to evaluate your own situation to see whether this technique is right for you.

Where should you borrow? Here's my order of preference for borrowing from lowest cost to highest cost:

1. Borrow from yourself and pay yourself interest. Take the money from your savings; let's say $2,000, as in Figure 9.9. Each month pay yourself $177.67 (put it into your savings) from your income that month. This payment includes an additional amount to cover the interest you lost on your initial withdrawal from savings.

2. If you have cash value in your life insurance, borrow against it. The interest rate on the loan probably will be lower than you could get elsewhere.

3. Get an interest-only loan against your certificates of deposit at your bank.

4. Get a simple interest loan.

If none of those are options, get an installment loan, which is usually more expensive than a simple interest loan. Shop around for the best rate and make sure there is no prepayment penalty.

## Other Investments

I know some of you are saying, "But what about other investments? I can't make high returns with these products." Yes, you can. Yields on quality bonds and mutual funds have been in the double digits. Money market funds keep up with rising inflation rates. You don't need to invest in other products unless you have plenty of money to spare and a high risk tolerance.

"But how can I impress my friends? These investments are so dull, they'll laugh at me!" Ah, now we get down to the real problem, that obstacle I mentioned in the Introduction: ego. Do you want to meet your goals or impress your friends? It's your money; no one cares more about it than you.

If you have extra money to invest after meeting your goals with my recommended investments, consider this story about other investments. Several years ago I spent almost a year researching investment diamonds. I read everything I could get my hands on and asked lots of questions. I went to the diamond markets. I talked to the buyers and sellers. In talking one day with a diamond broker, I asked his opinion on some diamonds I was considering buying. "Buy bonds," the diamond broker said. "They're safer."

## Individual Stocks

Don't invest in individual stocks unless you have at least $100,000 to invest. I'm definitely not against stocks. However, if you buy individual stocks and have less than $100,000, the transaction costs will wipe out any profit you might make, plus you won't be able to diversify enough.

Too many people get excited about the stock market because they hear others talking about the money they've made. But these people don't brag about the money they've lost in the market. Figure 9.10 shows a hypothetical example to make the point. In some years, the returns were great, up to 85 percent. But the down years dipped as low as −50 percent. The investor in this example had a real return of only 3.25 percent.

## Real Estate

Investment real estate—a category that doesn't include your own home—used to be a good investment. Its value depended on mortgage

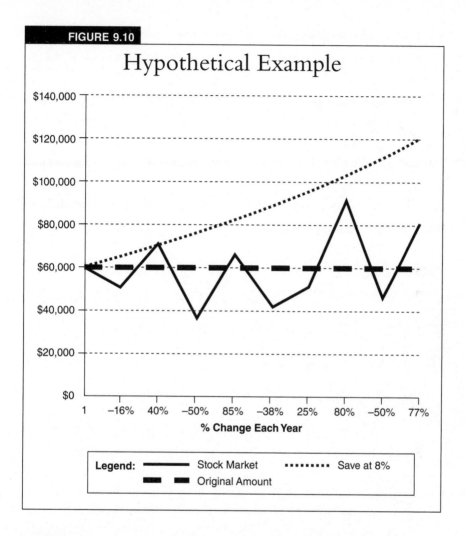

**FIGURE 9.10**

## Hypothetical Example

% Change Each Year:  1  −16%  40%  −50%  85%  −38%  25%  80%  −50%  77%

Legend: Stock Market · · · · · · · · Save at 8%
Original Amount

rates and the real estate market, as well as on the investor's willingness to put sweat equity into a project. As the business cycle and other factors change, the attractiveness of real estate as an investment changes.

If you are considering investing in real estate, compare the risk with CDs. What is a safe return with CDs? Can you get that same return with the property you are considering? Does your math consider maintenance, repairing damage, and paying the mortgage during times when you don't have a tenant?

Remember, too, that real estate has a tangible presence that many other investments lack—and that presence requires investor attention.

I use a two-hour rule. If you can't drive to it, don't buy it. You want to see it and keep an eye on it. This concept is valid no matter where you live.

If you consider real estate, don't buy glitz. Slick brochures don't necessarily mean a better deal. There are probably too many promotional costs and other overhead in big firms' deals.

When you buy real estate, buy a property, not an REIT. Again, you're buying real estate to diversify. In general, I'm not in favor of REITs for the same reason I don't recommend bond funds. You should buy a single product, not a pool of products.

## Commodities

Commodities, such as pork bellies or precious metals, are only for professionals. Some people are tempted by commodities' glamour, such as it is. Resist that temptation and don't trade commodities. You can meet your goals without them.

## Gold

Buy gold itself, not paper. Take physical possession of the gold.

## Collectibles

This category includes coins, art, and so on. Become an expert in whatever you plan to collect or don't bother. Remember that an investment is something you plan to sell, not a collection you build for your own pleasure. Also keep in mind that this is a very risky area. Today's Beanie Babies can be tomorrow's Cabbage Patch dolls, and it's easy to lose your investment when a particular artist or era goes out of style.

## Annuities

I don't care what the salespeople tell you, an annuity is not an investment. It should be a tool. Chapter 8 offers a discussion of annuities.

## Conclusion

Remember that there are many different schools of thought about how to invest. I've explained the concepts that I feel are time-tested and easy to use while keeping your time commitment and risk at a level that lets you sleep at night. Some of you will choose higher risk than others. Do what is right for you based on your finances and your temperament. You can still manage to be wealthy with conservative investments.

## Summary

1. Pay yourself first, beginning in January. Don't wait until later in the year to catch up on your savings. You'll lose a substantial sum in compounded interest.

2. Avoid leakage by always reinvesting the interest you earn.

3. Understand the basic financial cycle. When inflation and interest rates go up, businesses can't afford to borrow and the stock market goes down. Use money market funds to keep up with the rising rates.

4. When interest rates go down, businesses and individuals borrow and the stock market goes up. Lock in higher rates through long-term bonds.

5. Never be totally out of a product that you envision wanting at some time.

6. Try to beat inflation by 2 percent each year after taxes. That is your real return.

7. Learn the different types of financial risk and evaluate your risk tolerance.

# CHAPTER 10

# How to Find and Work with a Financial Planner

## Tyler V. Cook

The clients came in the door with looks of panic and desperation on their faces. They were drowning in debt. "What do we do?" they asked. "We feel like we make good money, but we're living paycheck to paycheck."

Without quite realizing it, they had already taken the single biggest step toward sorting out their finances. At age 26, they were sitting in a financial planner's office—a move that showed me that they understood the long-term impact today's decisions will have on their future.

If you're reading this book, you realize the same thing. The decisions you make now help determine the choices you'll have in the years to come. If your finances are simple and you are good at motivating and monitoring yourself, you can use this book to help create and stick to a financial plan that will maximize the work your money can do for you.

But if your finances are more complex and you might benefit from regular financial ideas and coaching, a good financial planner can be the difference between moderate success and slam-dunk financial management.

## What Is a Financial Planner?

As discussed in the book's introduction, a financial planner is your financial coach, the conductor of your financial orchestra, the coxswain of your financial rowing crew, the stage manager of your financial theater,

171

the general contractor of your financial building project, and the chef of your financial kitchen. You and your planner are in charge. You call in experts—insurance specialists, accountants, attorneys—as necessary, but you and your planner call the shots.

Do not put a specialist in a planner's job! The financial world is flooded with so-called advisors looking to make a quick buck by selling unnecessary products, rather than providing long-term financial planning services and growing with their clients. We also see insurance agents, CPAs, and attorneys who have honest intentions in marketing themselves as financial planners. Hiring them for the job is like asking your podiatrist to serve as your family doctor.

For one thing, there's a conflict of interest. An insurance agent can't take a truly disinterested look at your insurance needs when the agent gets paid when you buy insurance. Nor, for that matter, can a financial planner who works on commission, getting paid every time you buy a financial product, or a planner who earns a combination of fees and commissions keep your best interest front and center.

In addition, specialists such as insurance agents and accountants simply don't have the skills they would need to create and manage your entire financial plan. Their areas of expertise are important, but they don't have enough overlap with financial planners to do a financial planner's job.

Your best bet is a fee-only financial planner. Because you pay the fee-only planner a flat or hourly sum, she or he works for you, not for the companies that offer financial products. Fee-only planners have a fiduciary duty to act in your best interests only, not their own.

A fee-only financial planner—not a fee-based planner, who double dips by earning both fees and commissions—can help you navigate the maze of financial choices by giving you expert, unbiased advice. Don't assume what kind of planner you're meeting. Ask how the planner is compensated and what fiduciary requirements he or she has. If the answers aren't "from client fees only" and "an absolute fiduciary requirement to put my clients' interests first," find another planner.

We often see the results of hiring planners who don't put their clients' interests front and center. One of our clients, a woman in her late sixties, had previously worked with a family friend who was also a financial planner. As we soon found out, he was nothing more than a disguised insurance salesman. As I learned about her current financial situation, I noticed that she had a life insurance policy with a long-term care rider. Further exploration and discussion showed that the client had no need for either life insurance or long-term care insurance. Why did she have it? "My old advisor said I needed it," my client said. "He said I was getting older and I needed to buy long-term care insurance in case I needed to enter a nursing home in the future."

Why would a certified financial planner tell her that she needed life insurance when it was so obvious that she didn't? The answer was simple: greed. The client's annual life insurance premium was more than $19,000, and she had already paid three years of premiums when she began working with us. The planner kept a substantial portion of that sum as a commission. He took an additional $40,000 commission when he added the long-term care rider to the client's life insurance policy.

The financial planner had deliberately misled the client, which didn't sit well with me or with John Sestina. Along with a local independent insurance agent, we drafted a letter to the state insurance board explaining the situation. A few months later the client received a check from the insurance company for $86,762, returning her premiums and part of the commission she had wrongfully paid.

When you start your financial plan with the wrong advice, you pay for it later, and if you're like many people, you lack the knowledge you would need to evaluate what strategies and choices are right for you, at which stages of your life. Should you contribute to your company's 401(k) plan? Do you need an IRA? How much life insurance do you need, if you need life insurance at all? How much income tax should you withhold from your paycheck? What about disability insurance? Do I need estate-planning documents?

These questions barely scratch the surface of the topics comprehensive financial planning addresses. Without a planner to guide them, many people become overwhelmed, so they freeze. Don't fall victim to financial paralysis.

## Exposing the Myths

What are the other reasons that people don't make financial plans?

- **They think they have plenty of time.** When I ask younger people if they have financial plans in place, the most common answer is, "Why do I need a financial plan? I've got plenty of time to plan for my retirement. I'll worry about it when I'm older." That's dangerous. The longer you wait, the more excuses you find, and you never end up getting around to doing what needs to be done.

  Delay is expensive, too. If you start saving $5,500 a year at age 23 and earn an average annual return of 8 percent, you'll have more than $1,650,000 saved by age 65. Wait until age 30 to start saving, and that seven-year hesitation will cost your retirement portfolio more than $725,000.

- **They're too busy.** Everybody's busy, but most Americans brush their teeth before bed, because they've decided that clean, healthy teeth are important. You make time for the things you value. Regular updates with a financial planning professional should be one of those things.

- **They can't afford a financial planner.** Some people think financial planning is only for the wealthy or for those nearing retirement. That's wrong. No matter where you are in your life, you can benefit from expert financial advice, often for less than what some people spend on lattes every year.

Two of my clients, a married couple, were just 27 years old when we met. They had substantial student loan debt, limited income, and a negative net worth. Seven years later, they're in their mid-thirties and worth more than $1 million. The change didn't happen overnight, but they're well on their way to achieving their short-term and long-term goals. If they stay disciplined, their assets will continue to grow beyond what they imagined was possible seven years ago.

# How to Find a Financial Planner

Look for a fee-only planner who shares your mind-set, philosophies, and ideologies. You don't need to share political or religious views, but the client-planner relationship is far more productive when each party thinks similarly about money. You still won't always agree, but you'll speak one another's language.

Connecting with your advisor should feel natural, comfortable, and relaxing. If you're struggling to communicate or can't imagine talking about the private details of your life with a prospective advisor, then you might be better off with a different planner.

Existing clients and their families and friends refer most of our new clients to us. Consider asking your friends and family if they would recommend their planners.

## Do Your Research

CFP.net, letsmakeaplan.org, NAPFA.org (John Sestina is a founding member), and FPAnet.org are all places to find out more about potential planners, or to find potential planners in your geographic area.

When you find a planner who might fit you well, request a potential client meeting. Much as with dating, this is where the planner and potential client have an opportunity to make a first impression and to get to know each other. Treat it like an interview. If you agree to work together, what does the planner hope to have done for you in a year? In five years? Do your goals and expectations match?

Ask the planner how he or she is compensated. As I discussed earlier, many planners say that they're fee-based, which typically means that they charge clients low-ball fees and make most of their money by selling products. This is a frequent point of confusion. You want a fee-only planner: someone who is compensated solely through client fees, not through commissions.

Most clients prefer working with well-established planners. If the planner is relatively new to the field, ask for more information on the company's history and support staff. When I was starting my career, John Sestina attended every meeting with me until I was seasoned enough to run meetings alone. I now mentor younger planners, just as John mentored me. Keep in mind that some older advisors haven't kept up with new ideas about technology and practice management. (There are exceptions, of course. John is the most tech-savvy older person I've ever met.)

We encourage potential clients to work with a certified financial planner (CFP).

A CFP must pass a rigorous exam, have three years of industry experience, and maintain their certification through ongoing continuing education. I don't believe that CFP accreditation automatically makes someone a better planner, but it does show a high level of commitment to both learning and ethics.

Your planner should be a fiduciary. All CFPs are mandatory fiduciaries, putting client interests ahead of their own.

Is your prospective planner a member of the National Association of Personal Financial Advisors (NAPFA)? Are they dedicated to fee-only compensation? Some advisors claim to wear multiple hats: sometimes a CFP, other times an insurance agent, and so on. I believe it shouldn't be both. Either you're always providing unbiased advice, which I believe can only be done by foregoing commissions, or you're not.

Do you need a specialized financial planner? Some business owners, people with non–U.S. citizenship, or clients with significant foreign assets, among others, may get better guidance from a planner who is particularly familiar with their particular challenges. Perhaps you're a business owner and you'd like to work with a planner who is knowledgeable in tax planning for small businesses. Over time, planners tend to specialize in certain industries as their client bases grow.

This is a tricky subject. In some cases, working with a planner who specializes in certain areas may not be the best approach. You want a planner who is knowledgeable in all aspects of finance and who knows where to look and who to ask when additional expertise is needed. As I've said, if you're the owner of a football team, your financial planner is the coach, deploying specialists—quarterback, linebackers, physical therapists—as necessary to reach the teams' overall goals.

## Keep in Touch

How much contact does your prospective planner expect to have with you?

Communication is key to any relationship, and the relationship between planner and client is no exception. We are proactive and in constant communication with our financial planning clients. In fact, John Sestina gets upset if a client has to ask a question, because he feels the planner should have anticipated the question and already answered it. He admits this is a bit extreme, but it gives insight into our attitude as a company.

If your planner charges hourly fees, you may be hesitant to get in touch when you have a question or an issue. You're more likely to keep a planner up to date on your progress and life changes if the planner charges a flat fee—and the information you offer helps your planner do better work for you.

## Work the Plan

After you've found the right financial planner for you and laid the foundation of your work together, you'll continue to develop your relationship. We've had clients for 50 years; the service doesn't stop until the client's death, and even then, the planner can be instrumental in helping the family execute the will and manage the estate. I've become friends with many of my clients, and I'm often the first person clients tell about their big news: engagement, marriage, divorce, job promotion, pregnancy.

Remember that the most successful clients are those who remember the acronym KISS: keep it simple, stupid. The U.S. Navy enshrined the KISS design principle in the 1960s, noting that most systems work best if they are kept simple, not complicated. This principle holds true for most financial plans. Too often, people are knocked off course by an idea they hear at the water cooler or the country club or by a fear-motivated sales pitch. Even with a good plan, making progress takes time. Keep the faith.

# CHAPTER 11

# Financial Planning for Women

## *Kimberly E. Wirtz*

Although the basic tenets of financial planning are gender neutral, women face many unique issues when it comes to their financial plans.

Most women spend a portion of their adult lives living alone. This could be due to divorce, a spouse's death, a choice to remain single, or a variety of other reasons, but being alone is something for which every woman should plan.

Women tend to outlive men. My mother is 78 and in great health physically and mentally. My father passed away and after 45 years of marriage, my mother found herself alone. She had never taken out the trash. She did not pay the bills. She did not make decisions about insurance or maintain her vehicles. She did not cut the grass, shovel snow, or repair things in the house when they broke. These were all things my father did and all things my mother had to take over and learn, or relearn, when she was in her seventies.

Statistics show that 80 percent of women die single and 80 percent of men die married. Because most women will spend some of their life alone, women should prepare for this eventuality. Particularly in older generations, married women often allowed their husbands to run the family finances. Back in the day, it was normal to divide work into men's jobs and women's jobs. It was a man's duty to provide for his family, make sure there was enough money, and take care of the finances. The woman ran the home, kept it clean, and raised the children. This arrangement may have been an efficient division of chores, but it wasn't—and isn't—a good way for both spouses to learn about handling financial matters.

## Learn About Family Finances While You Can

Because wives so frequently relinquish financial control, women are often in the dark about basic details: where the family money is located, how much there is, how much the family spends on routine monthly expenses, whether there is a retirement plan or a pension, who the beneficiaries of the life insurance policies or retirement plans are. She has been perfectly content to let her husband handle the finances. I often hear "I am not good at that," "I don't know anything about money or investing," and "I don't want to know anything about that and I am happy to let Bob handle the money." That's great—until the husband becomes disabled, gets Alzheimer's disease, divorces the wife, or dies. Then what?

You can prevent a great deal of stress by familiarizing yourself with the family finances before circumstances force you to do so. I have a client who came to see me when her husband was in the beginning stages of Alzheimer's. They had been married for 60 years, and for 60 years he had handled the finances. Fortunately, he was fairly organized and kept a lot of the original investment paperwork, which helped us locate accounts and determine cost basis. We found investment accounts scattered at various brokerage firms. He had several IRA accounts and taxable accounts in addition to stock certificates dating back to 1965. He was receiving a pension from his former employer. He chose the 100 percent joint and survivor annuity, so that his wife would get the same annuity payment for the rest of her life if he died first. He made sure she was taken care of.

When they came to see me, he was still able to recall enough information to help our discovery process. What if they had not come to me in time? He may not have remembered where all of his assets were located. We may have overlooked an account that was not properly titled and caused a trip to probate because we did not know the account existed or where to find it. All of those IRAs would have been a nightmare to inherit, even with the wife named as beneficiary. Because he was still able to communicate and comprehend, we were able to find all the assets, ensure everything was properly titled, and consolidate all those IRAs into one. Having only one IRA made taking his required distribution much easier; it will also make it much easier to pass the IRA to the wife at the husband's death.

The stock certificates were in the husband's name only, and there was no provision for them to pass to his wife at his death. He did have a will, drawn up more than 25 years ago, that left the stock to his wife. A judge must read a will. Finding a judge means going to probate court, a trip that also requires an attorney. All of that costs money, takes time, is public, and is unpleasant, especially for someone who is already grieving. I have clients who have been tied up in probate for more than two years. I also knew a very wealthy man who died suddenly at the age of 50 without an estate plan. His estate was tied up in probate for more than 15 years. When all was finally settled, very little of his money remained for his beneficiaries. His private financial life was made very public and his family spent a great deal of those 15 years in court battling for what could have easily passed to them with proper estate planning.

For the client in the beginning stages of Alzheimer's disease, we added a transfer-on-death provision to the stock certificate, which means that at his death, the stock transfers automatically, by law. That will let his family avoid probate. They won't need a judge to read the will and figure out who will get the asset. A transfer-on-death provision overrides the will, as do beneficiary designations. We also updated the couples' wills and powers of attorney, not only so the wife could step in and make decisions on behalf of her declining husband, but also so that some-one could be named to act on her behalf, as her husband could no longer do so.

Perhaps most important, in the three years they have been clients, she has become comfortable working with me and understands her financial plan. His disease has unfortunately progressed, but because they sought help from a financial planner before he became incompetent, we could help prepare his wife for being alone. When the time comes, she can mourn her husband and not stress over how to handle his estate.

## Understand Your Assets, Where They Are, and Who Legally Owns Them

Married women should have a basic, general knowledge of their family financial situation. They should know what assets they have and who legally owns them. Are any assets—house, cars, boats, bank accounts, and investments—individually owned? If so, consider either owning them jointly or adding a transfer-on-death provision to avoid probate and to allow the surviving spouse immediate access to assets and funds. Banks freeze individually owned assets at death, making potentially needed funds unavailable to the surviving spouse.

If the couple owns an asset in a community property state, the full value of the asset may not automatically go to the surviving spouse. The surviving spouse may only be entitled to half the asset, leaving the other half up for grabs and necessitating a trip to probate court. You can avoid this by titling assets as community property with rights of survivorship, so that when one spouse dies the other automatically inherits the full value of the community property.

A married woman should know where all the marital assets are located. When a spouse relinquishes financial control, it is much easier for the partner to hide money or open accounts without the spouse's knowledge. This can make it very difficult to find assets in case of divorce, death, or disability.

Many people use safe deposit boxes to keep their valuables and important documents, a list that often includes wills. If the box is rented in one spouse's name and something happens to that spouse, the partner will not be able to access the will and other contents without an order from the probate court. Consider renting a safe deposit box jointly with your spouse, so that at the first death, the surviving spouse will have immediate access to the contents.

## Consolidate Accounts

Perhaps 85 percent of my new clients have assets scattered all over the place. Consider consolidating accounts. It is so much easier to keep track of what you own when it is all in one place. You don't need checking accounts at three banks or four IRAs at four different brokerage firms. One of each will do. Federal Deposit Insurance Corporation (FDIC) deposit insurance insures individual accounts at one bank for up to $250,000. However, a married couple with joint accounts gets $250,000 in insurance coverage for each joint account owner, letting them insure $500,000. If each member of the couple has an individual account with a transfer-on-death provision, each of those accounts is also insured up to $250,000. In total, a married couple can insure $1 million through FDIC coverage—a generously sufficient level for most of my clients and enough to make additional accounts at other banks unnecessary.

Brokerage accounts offer coverage against brokerage failure, though not against investment losses or broker misconduct. Instead of FDIC insurance, brokerage accounts are insured through the Securities Investor Protection Corporation (SIPC). The upper coverage limit is $500,000, with a $250,000 allowance for cash. Many brokerage firms carry additional insurance through Lloyd's of London, providing account holders with supplemental protection of up to $150 million in assets and cash of $1.15 million. This makes having accounts at several brokerage firms unnecessary for most people.

In addition, owning several retirement accounts makes passing those accounts to the intended beneficiary much more cumbersome and time-consuming than owning only one, and can also delay the beneficiary's access to the funds. Having more than one account makes it easier to lose track of an account; it also makes it more difficult to properly allocate your investments. When it's time to begin taking required minimum distributions from all of those scattered retirement accounts, the process becomes burdensome. If you overlook an account, the penalty for not taking your required minimum distribution is stiff: 50 percent of the distribution will go to the IRS! For most people, consolidating accounts is best.

## Name Primary and Backup Beneficiaries

If you are a married, your spouse must name you as the primary beneficiary of any qualified retirement plan unless you agree, in writing, to let your spouse name someone else. A problem often arises when a person divorces and does not change the beneficiary to someone other than the former spouse or remarries but does not update the beneficiary designation. The beneficiary designation trumps everything else. Even if your divorce decree says your ex gets nothing, if the ex is still named as an account beneficiary, the ex gets the money. Without a properly named beneficiary, you could create an unintended windfall for your former spouse.

Even with a properly named, primary beneficiary, it's wise to name a backup beneficiary. This ensures that money will go to the intended heir if you and your beneficiary die at the same time or your beneficiary predeceases you.

## Understand Pension and Social Security Arrangements

A married woman should also know whether her spouse has a pension and, if so, what will happen when her spouse dies. Does the pension payment stop or will the surviving spouse continue to get pension payments? How much and for how long?

We have a client who chose a single life annuity for his pension payout when he retired at age 62. His wife had been a homemaker and had no retirement accounts and little Social Security income. They did not have enough investment assets to take care of her if he died prematurely and the pension stopped. The wiser decision would have been for him to select a joint and survivor annuity, which would have continued the pension payments to his wife after his death. It's too late to choose that option, so now they will likely have to insure his life to provide income for her. At his age and health, life insurance will be very expensive.

Social Security is another potential pitfall for a married woman. If a woman's spouse takes Social Security too soon, reducing the payout amount, the spouse could limit the wife to a lifetime of less income than she would have if the spouse had waited to take Social Security at the normal retirement age (or even older). Waiting to collect Social Security at the normal retirement age gives the surviving spouse an annual increase of 8 percent, and that adds up over a lifetime.

A woman who divorces after having been married for at least 10 years may qualify to collect benefits based on her ex's Social Security record. She is entitled to collect on her ex-spouse's Social Security benefit—even if the ex remarries, and even if the new spouse collects on the ex's record. If she remarries and that marriage ends, she may still be able to collect benefits from the ex-spouse's Social Security record. If the former spouse has died, she may also be able to collect survivor's benefits from the ex-spouse's Social Security account, even if she is remarried.

## You Need a Will, a Living Will, and Two Powers of Attorney

Every adult should have essential estate-planning documents: a will, a living will, a healthcare power of attorney, and a financial or durable power of attorney. If a woman is married and her spouse cannot make independent medical decisions, she doesn't automatically get to make those decisions for him just because she is his spouse. Some states only require that a doctor consult with the next of kin. Next of kin could be the spouse but could also be an adult child or children. Some states let doctors choose the decision maker from a list based on whom the physician believes is best suited to the job: a parent, a spouse, or a child. A doctor who disagrees with the spouse could choose someone else. There does not have to be agreement. What if the adult children disagree with the spouse? What if the spouse is a second wife and doctors grant her husband's children from his first marriage the authority to make decisions on his behalf? Or what if the spouse knows her husband did not want to be kept alive artificially, but his children think she is trying to kill their father? An ugly battle often ensues.

Like probate, these battles can be costly, time consuming, and public. If you take the time to plan now, you can make sure that the person you choose will be the one making decisions on your behalf if you are unable to do so. Remember the client with Alzheimer's? He had all his estate documents drawn up and current before his decline began. That would not have been possible after he became unable to make his own decisions.

These documents and directives are especially important for a single woman, because there is no spouse to act as her agent if she becomes unable to make decisions on her own. I am an only child and a single woman. If I do not name someone to make decisions for me if I become incapacitated, who will have that responsibility? Who will pay my bills if I'm in a coma? A durable power of attorney would let someone write checks on my behalf. When you give someone a healthcare power of attorney or a financial power of attorney, that person can act as if she were you. Choose someone you trust implicitly.

## Both Spouses Need Life and Disability Insurance

A female homemaker with children needs to make sure her working spouse has a life insurance policy that would provide income to her should he die. There are many factors to consider when deciding how much life insurance you need. How old are the children? What kind of education do you want to provide for them? Does that include college? Paying off debts? Will the surviving spouse return to work? If so, when will the spouse begin working and who will take care of the kids? How much will childcare cost? It's a tragedy to lose a spouse, but an even bigger tragedy if the children who lost a father also lose a mother because she has to work two jobs to keep a roof over her family's head. Life insurance gives the family time to grieve and heal by eliminating worries about funding college and paying the mortgage.

A homemaker should also have life insurance. In her absence, someone would have to take over caring for the children and the home. The national average salary for a full-time nanny is almost $40,000 per year. A cleaning service can cost between $50 and $100 per visit. A personal shopper can cost as much as $15,000 per year and meal preparation another $13,000 annually. If the homemaker manages the family finances, add another $5,000 annually. The total—more than $75,000 per year—is a very conservative estimate of what it would cost to hire someone to take over a homemaker's job.

The same wife and mother must make sure her working spouse has sufficient disability insurance, too. A long-term disability can financially devastate a family. A single woman should also ensure she has sufficient disability insurance. A good friend of mine had a disastrous fall and shattered her pelvis and hips. She had short-term disability through work but did not opt for long-term disability coverage because she would have had to pay for the benefit. She was forced to go back to work before her recovery was complete, which will likely cause her a lifetime of pain.

Another woman I know worked as a consultant after many years as a public employee. She was out on a bike ride when a tree cracked and fell on top of her, paralyzing her from the neck down. She was in her forties and had never thought to purchase a disability policy. Fortunately, her years of public service qualified her for disability benefits through her former employer. The benefits allowed her to make her home wheelchair accessible and to pay her bills, even though she could not work, and let her new husband take a year off of work to help with her recovery. She was able to focus on getting better and has since regained movement in her legs, allowing her to walk short distances. Today she travels the country and speaks on the importance of adequate disability insurance.

Because women tend to live longer than men, wives also run into issues with long-term care. A woman might nurse her spouse through his final illness, but who cares for her when she is sick? Who looks after a single woman who can't care for herself? Long-term care costs may also be higher for women, because women tend to live longer and so often spend more time receiving care. Long-term care insurance can help provide this cost, but the policies are becoming more and more expensive, and the benefit periods are being reduced. Planning and saving for this expense is a necessity.

Women also have the challenge of competing financial needs and expectations. Women who work for pay tend to earn less than their male counterparts. They may take breaks from the workforce to raise a family and may also have the responsibility of caring for aging parents. Being able to work fewer hours, and receiving less pay for those hours than their male counterparts, means that women have an especially hard time saving for their own financial needs. Providing care for an aging parent, putting kids through college, saving for their retirement, and being adequately insured can easily become overwhelming, competing priorities.

Women also tend to be less confident about investing. They tend to think more about security than about growth. In a world where risk is rewarded, this leads them to invest too conservatively to meet their retirement needs. It is harder to save for retirement when you are earning less than your male counterparts, investing too conservatively, raising your kids, taking in young adult children who have returned to the nest, and caring for aging parents. It is harder to save for retirement when you live longer than men and thus have to make your money last longer.

## Balancing It All

Women who seek my financial advice are looking for ways to balance it all. They want help but are often overwhelmed when they seek it. Unfortunately, financial advisors intimidate many women, even very successful career women. They often find that advisors, especially male advisors, are condescending. Many women have similar expectations of male financial planners, car salesmen, and mechanics: experience suggests that the men will talk down to them and take advantage of them by selling them products they don't need. Because of this, women tend to avoid working with financial planners or stop working with their planners shortly after they begin. Many of my female clients came to me because I am a woman.

Women face many unique financial planning challenges, but proper planning and attention to detail can help them avoid many pitfalls. Like the commercial says, "Life comes at you fast." By preparing for the many curveballs life can toss your way, you can get on with the business of living. Proper planning brings peace of mind.

# CHAPTER 12

# Financial Planning for Business Owners

### Stephen Lukan

One of our clients, a young professional woman, was doing the daily grind of corporate America. Her husband had a steady job that brought in enough money to pay their bills. She decided to take a shot as a real estate agent, as she had always had an interest in this industry. She established her business with assistance from a CPA, got her real estate license, and was off and running. With determination and hard work, she quickly created a successful business. The couple didn't increase their lifestyle, so they were able to live off the husband's income and save most of her income in a retirement plan.

We brought in a third-party administrator to discuss retirement plan options and decided on a profit-sharing plan with an attached 401(k), which lets our client deposit most of her income in a tax-deferred retirement account. Her income continued to grow, so we asked the third-party administrator to reevaluate the situation and then added a defined-benefit plan. Now the couple is on track to achieve financial independence by their mid-fifties.

As this story illustrates, owning a business can bring both tangible and intangible benefits: extra income, a sense of accomplishment, freedom to be your own boss, tax benefits, and retirement savings tools.

Though the world contains a plethora of different business types, they divide into two basic kinds: businesses that provide a primary source of income and businesses that provide a secondary income source, which are also known as hobby businesses. Sometimes a hobby business becomes such a success that it turns into the owner's primary source of income.

## Business Structure

Corporate structure helps define any business's operation and taxation. Possible structures include:

- **Sole proprietorship.** This is an easy choice for an individual or married couple running a simple business. It's easy to create a sole proprietorship—just check the correct box on your tax forms—and report your taxes on the Schedule C form. You can deduct business expenses and are personally liable for your company's debts and errors. If you're new to having your own business and plan to start out small, this is probably a fine corporate structure for you. It's easy to change in the future.

- **S corporation.** An S corporation is another choice for small businesses. It's a flow-through entity, which is a fancy way of saying that the business doesn't pay taxes. Instead, the firm's shareholders divide the company's gains and losses and report those on their individual income tax returns. To qualify for S corporate status, your firm must not have more than 100 shareholders, must have only individuals as shareholders, must not have a nonresident alien as a shareholder, and must have only one class of stock.

- **C corporation.** S corporations tax income once, at the individual level. C corporations, on the other hand, tax income twice: once at the corporate level and again at the individual level, when the corporation distributes profits. The trade-off is that C corporations can be much bigger and have no restrictions on the number, nationality, or residence of their shareholders.

- **General partnership.** In a general partnership, two or more people share in a company's profits, losses, and management. Each partner is equally and personally liable for the firm's debts.

- **Limited partnership.** Limited partnerships are composed of one or more general partners, who manage the business, and one or more limited partners, who share in the firm's profits but are only liable up to the amount of their investment in the company.

- **Limited liability company, or LLC.** An LLC is a sort of hybrid, combining qualities of both the S and C corporate structures. Like an S corporation, it's a pass-through entity, so profits are taxed just once, at the individual level. Like a C corporation, it places no limits on the number or type of owners. Only an LLC's company assets are at risk in case of liability.

A discussion of all the ins and outs of these corporate structures is outside the scope of this book. Talk with an attorney who specializes in this area of law if you suspect your business may benefit from having more than the simplest corporate structure.

## Turning a Hobby into a Business

To start a business, entrepreneurs often look to their passions. Find something you love to do and see whether you can persuade someone to pay you to do it.

Your interests and imagination are the only limiting factors on the list of possibilities, which might include photography, computers and information technology, interior decorating, sewing, jewelry design and manufacture, personal training, or textile design.

You'll need a name for your business, business cards, a website, a dedicated computer (if appropriate), and a bank account. Banks offer business accounts, of course, but charge for them. A separate personal account that's used strictly for business purposes, on the other hand, is typically both free and acceptable to the IRS.

In addition to those items, you'll need to do a substantial amount of research. Can you afford any capital outlay your business will require? Will you need to spend money on marketing? Will you still enjoy your passion when it's something you've promised other people that you'll do?

Perhaps most important, is there a market for your goods or services? Look around for other, similar businesses. Are they doing well? Do you see a market niche that they haven't yet exploited? Dip a toe into the business waters by selling a small quantity of whatever your business will sell. Was it relatively easy to find someone who wanted to buy your offering? This is the time to find another plan if you find little or no market. Prospective business owners often spend a lot of time deciding on the perfect business name and putting just the right people on their boards of directors. All those details are unimportant compared to making sure that people want to buy what you want to sell.

## Tax and Retirement Planning

As you consider whether your prospective firm is financially viable, remember that having a business has both tax and retirement planning advantages.

First, the U.S. government offers tax incentives, loans, and grants to encourage business development. Many of these incentives are available to even the smallest companies. The Small Business Administration (SBA, www.sba.gov) is a good place to begin learning about your options.

Second, many expenses that are not normally tax deductible become deductible when they're used for business purposes. The list includes home office expenses such as rent and utilities, computer equipment, books, training, cell phones, and Internet access, as well as raw materials and items for resale. Travel costs are tax deductible. Combine business with pleasure and deduct the business portion of any trip.

Again, tax code particulars can change, and their details are beyond the scope of this book. Consult your tax advisor on specific tax provisions and deductions (see Table 12.1).

A business of your own also gives you related retirement plan options: SIMPLE IRA, SEP IRA, 401(k), a pension plan, and a profit-sharing plan. All these plans let you save pretax dollars, which lowers your current income tax bill and gives you more money to invest, hastening the day when you reach financial independence.

**TABLE 12.1**

# Salary Employee versus Business

|                                            | Salary Employee | Business   |
| ------------------------------------------ | --------------- | ---------- |
| Income                                     | $40,000         | $40,000    |
| Expenses                                   | $0              | ($5,000)   |
| Taxable income                             | $40,000         | $35,000    |
| Taxes paid @25% tax rate                   | ($10,000)       | ($8,750)   |
| Expenses (cell phone, computer, travel)    | ($5,000)        | $0         |

Depending on your business, you may also be able to hire family members and include them in your firm's retirement plan. A financial planner can help you choose the best plan type for your situation.

## Building a Team

In addition to helping you choose the best type of retirement plan for your company, the right financial advisor can help you combine your personal and business interests in the most advantageous ways. A good financial advisor may also give you business advice or introduce you to other helpful professionals.

The larger and more complex the business, the more help you'll need. In addition to a financial planner, your lineup might include a certified public accountant, an attorney, an insurance agent who can advise you on what coverage you need, and a retirement plan administrator. Though you may want to hire family as much as possible, it's important that you select expert professionals who can give you top-notch service and advice. Don't hire a CPA just because she's your daughter-in-law.

Ask the professionals who work with you on your company to point you toward an entrepreneurial mentorship group. Meeting regularly and with complete confidentiality, a mentorship group is a place where members can exchange advice and test ideas with business owners at various stages and from a variety of industries. The help you get here can make or break you.

## Business Partners

Depending on your company, you might want one or more business partners. When you start a business with someone, you essentially marry that person, with the expectation that you'll get along well, the business will thrive, and everyone involved will make money.

As we all know, however, marriages don't always work out; a prenuptial agreement can help protect the spouses in case of a divorce. In business, a similar document serves the same purpose. A buy-sell agreement lets you and your partner(s) decide what you'll do in case things don't go exactly as planned. As table 12.2 shows, you should consider and discuss what will happen if:

- You or your partner dies or becomes disabled
- An owner decides to retire, move to another city, or leave to start another business
- You and your partner can't get along
- A divorce settlement will award an ownership interest to a former spouse
- You receive an attractive offer from an outsider

**TABLE 12.2**

# Sole Proprietorship, Partnership or LLC, and Corporations (S or C)

| Business Form | Issue | How Buy-Sell Agreement Can Help |
|---|---|---|
| Sole Proprietorship | Heirs lack skills to operate business. | Assures a willing and knowledgeable buyer. |
| Partnership or LLC | Deceased partner's heirs may have immediate financial needs. | Provides a quicker estate settlement at a fair price. |
| Corporations (S or C) | Business may be threatened by heirs with different styles or interests. | Prevents remaining owners from losing control of business. |

- A partner retires
- A partner files for personal bankruptcy
- For any other reason, you need to determine the appropriate price for a partner's interest in the company

## Succession Planning

A buy-sell agreement is just part of an overall succession plan, which is a vitally important part of running many businesses. (A sole proprietorship that sells the owner's personal abilities as a computer programmer or designer may not need a succession plan, because no one else could run the business, and the firm has nothing to sell without its owner.)

Succession plans are like estate plans, in that some people avoid them because they associate such plans with the fact that all things must end. This is a mistake and on more than one level. First, you may someday want to walk away from your business because there is something else you want even more—a new business, time with another person, travel, or just a different kind of adventure.

Second, succession plans are absolutely crucial, particularly for successful firms. All businesses eventually change hands. A good succession plan helps a company's owner control when, how, and to whom the business will ultimately sell, as well as how that sale will benefit the owner, family members, and key employees. Plus, customers may feel at ease knowing a succession plan is in place.

Succession plans begin with a thorough company evaluation, one that looks at every aspect of the business: operations, staffing, capacity, growth, productivity, and profitability. In addition to creating a clear portrait of the company, the process also reveals problems that need to be addressed or areas that could be improved, leading the way to a more successful business in the here and now.

An evaluation can also point to ways that a business needs to adjust before it changes hands. These issues frequently have something to do with accounting. Maybe the business started small and still doesn't employ formal accounting procedures in keeping track of its profits and expenses. Perhaps the owner's personal finances are too tangled up with the business; a company car that's really a personal car or an owner who gets her weekend cash by dipping into the petty cash buckets are possible examples. There may be nothing illegal about these practices, but they stand in the way of a clear, accurate description of the firm's worth.

The company owner also needs to minimize the risk that the business will fail if he steps away. Train other people to do the work that you do. Write down the things you know.

A solid evaluation can also point to a firm's next logical owners. Key employees might take over, which would mean continuing a successful business model and assuming more responsibility.

The next generation of the owner's family might want to buy out the owner or inherit the company. In that case, it's important to keep business and sentiment as separate as possible, clearly communicating the deal and finding ways for children or grandchildren who will not inherit the company to inherit other assets of comparable worth. It's best not to force this solution onto a child or a grandchild. In my experience, either a person is interested in a particular kind of business or they have other dreams for themselves. It's not helpful or productive to pressure heirs to take over a business that they really don't want.

Selling a firm to a competitor or other company that would benefit by purchasing it is another possible succession plan. Maybe another firm is interested in having a similar business in a new area, or a different business owner could add your distribution company to her factory.

Private equity firms sometimes also buy privately held companies, usually to add some kind of value and then resell at a profit. Looking at the various options early is typically the best way to make sure that the business you worked hard to build continues, even after you're no longer at the helm.

# CHAPTER 13

# Financial Planning for Physicians

## *Bhagwan Satiani*

Physicians and other healthcare professionals, like other high earners, are much sought after by financial advisors. They are often referred to as *whales* because they are considered slow, easy targets who yield fat fees. Despite the often-substantial student loan debt they carry after finishing their training, physicians' potential income-earning ability puts a big target on their backs. Net worth increases with age. A recent survey indicated that by age 50, more than half, or 55 percent, of physicians have a net worth exceeding $1 million and by age 65, 49 percent accumulate more than $2 million.

Student debt is a large burden for most healthcare professionals. Eighty-four percent of 2014 public medical school graduates carried some debt; the mean was $176,348, a figure that doesn't count a median undergraduate debt of $20,000.

Most physicians, nurses, and other medical professionals receive almost no education or training in financial matters, including choosing financial advisors. Medical schools of all sorts focus on 10 or more years of medical education and training; few have any meaningful curricula related to personal finance. With no basic understanding of finance, physicians make mistakes. And once they've launched their medical careers, they don't have time to learn about finance or to correct their earlier errors.

# Reasons for Bad Financial Decisions

There are a variety of other reasons, too, that healthcare professionals are prone to making bad financial decisions:

1. **Ego.** They are experts in their area and been told they are very smart; they tend to consider themselves knowledgeable in financial matters by reading a book or two, by talking to misinformed friends, or by dubious websites.

2. **Expectations.** The average physician completes medical school at age 27 and often finishes residency after age 30. That's a long time to postpone entering the workforce, particularly while friends and classmates are working and making money, and it can give doctors a hastened drive toward wealth acquisition. When health professionals enter practice, they suddenly begin receiving large, regular paychecks, which feeds the pent-up demand. During year one as a fully qualified physician, for instance, a doctor might go from a median residency salary of $51,250 a year to $40,000 a month in some cases!

3. **Too little time.** Newly minted medical professionals are busy people, and financial planning is important but not urgent. Finding a financial advisor easily falls to the bottom of the list.

# Results of Financial Mistakes

Mistakes result—mistakes that tread on every basic tenet of sound financial planning. Results include the following.

## Insufficient Rainy-Day Funds

Given the gusher of money suddenly available, doctors' self-discipline goes out the window. They have a sense of entitlement and a long list of items on their wish lists; even otherwise sensible people lose their perspective. Healthcare professionals often think that, after their student debt is paid off and they've paid for cars, homes, and expensive vacations, there will be plenty of time to save for the unexpected. That isn't always the case.

With a saving rate around 12 percent, nurses are better savers than most Americans, who typically save around 10.5 percent of their incomes. But, even though 61 percent of physicians claim to live within their means, it's often hard to persuade doctors to set aside 15 percent or more of their net incomes.

## Infallibility

Doctors spend a lot of time learning how to be right, and they often share a sense of immortality with other young people. Catastrophes happen to other people, so they see no need to make life and disability insurance a priority, even though coverage for healthy people in their thirties is easy and relatively cheap. When they do buy insurance, they often choose the wrong benefit amount or buy policies that they don't need.

Individual circumstances dictate the need for insurance, as well as the benefit amount, price, tax consequences, and duration. (See Table 13.1.)

When young doctors are in training, someone often persuades them to buy a lot of whole life insurance and a low-deductible car insurance policy. Like most people in their thirties, however, they vastly underestimate their need for disability insurance.

Consider the odds of becoming disabled. The chance of dying prematurely is 1 in 117, but most of us buy life insurance. According to data from Cornell University, the odds of losing your car is 1 in 160, but the odds of becoming disabled from injury or illness is 1 in 9 for people between the ages of 21 and 65. Physicians and other healthcare professionals get into their prime working years between the ages of 35 and 65, when the odds of disability increase to 1 in 7. The *McGill Advisory* reports that although most physicians have a disability policy, 40 percent have group or association policies, which provide much lower benefits than do individual policies.

| TABLE 13.1 | | |
|---|---|---|

# Comparison of Term and Whole Life Insurance Policies

| | **Term Policy** | **Whole Life Policy** |
|---|---|---|
| Duration | Limited, specified | Death benefit and cash value |
| Cash value | None | Savings accumulate; guaranteed cash value |
| Initial payments for same coverage | Significantly less than a whole life policy | Significantly more than a term life policy |
| Benefits | Only if death occurs during coverage period | Guaranteed coverage for life |
| Borrowing against cash value | No | Yes, with specified interest rate |
| Accelerated benefits option for terminal illness | Maybe | Maybe |
| Waiver of premium | Available | Available |
| Cost of premiums | Same with level term, with an increase for annual renewability | Depends on policy |
| Income-tax advantages | None | Yes |
| Investment returns | Can be significant | Low |
| Evidence of insurability | On purchase (if over a certain amount) and for annual renewable policies | On purchase |

## Waiting to Save for Retirement

In a study of 2.6 million Americans eligible for a 401(k) or other defined-contribution plan, Hewitt Associates reported that 72 percent were putting their money into a 401(k), and 81 percent had a separate retirement savings account, though the median 401(k) balance in a 401(k) was only $40,730 for men and $18,130 for women.

In general, physicians put away more for retirement than the average American, but their savings may still not be enough to fund a comfortable retirement. Many physicians and other professionals do not contribute consistently to retirement funds. Not enough physicians take advantage of defined-contribution plans because of IRS limits on contribution limits. They often save only enough to replace 56 percent of their pre-retirement income, in contrast to a suggested replacement goal of 71 percent.

Because of a progressive approach to high-income earners, physicians don't benefit as much as the rest of the population from Social Security benefits. Social Security may only replace between 10 percent and 20 percent of high ending salaries, in contrast to 30 percent to 40 percent of average salaries. High earners need a higher savings rate as they plan for retirement, compared to average income earners. But only 40 percent of physicians under age 50 contribute up to their defined-contribution plan limits, whereas 70 percent of physicians above age 50 reach the limit and made catch-up contributions.

Nonqualified plans are a viable option for physicians and other high-income healthcare professionals. A 457(b) plan is one possibility. But younger physicians underuse such plans. Seventy-four percent of physicians earning more than $500,000 use nonqualified plans, compared to just 6 percent of physicians earning less than $150,000.

## Wrong Asset Allocation Strategies

Between their delayed workforce entry and tendency to overspend, healthcare professionals often feel pressure to make up for lost time in saving for retirement. That can push them to take inappropriate risks: investment strategies that are too aggressive or proposed by advisors looking to make a quick profit.

Physicians have very low unemployment rates and typically generate steady incomes for many decades. Over a long period of time, equities generate higher returns than do other investment vehicles, so it stands to reason that physicians in their early thirties can afford to take a bit more risk by allocating a good percentage of their savings to equities. On the other hand, as people get older and head into retirement, most advisors agree that it's time to consider less aggressive strategies.

Yet 42 percent of physicians age 60 to 64 have portfolios that are more than 64 percent equities.

## The High Cost of Investing

Average mutual fund fees—also called loads—have gone down by 75 percent since 1990. Compared to no-load funds, however, they still represent a burden over a long period of time. This is partly because many investors have moved their money into no-load index funds, institutional no-load shares, or choose no-load options through retirement funds but also shows a real decline in individual equity funds. Wrap accounts or asset-based fees, which are assessed as a percentage of assets under management, carry lower fees. However, fees tend to remain high for sector funds invested in real estate or in high-growth or emerging-market stocks.

If your investment costs are 1 percent, 2 percent, or even 3 percent a year, that comes straight off the top of your return. Costs of 3 percent a year reduce an after-inflation return of 5 percent to 2 percent. After 35 years of saving $50,000 a year, that's a difference of $2 million, or more than all the money you saved over those years! Taxes on your investment returns can have exactly the same effect, so it is important to minimize those as much as possible, too. (See Table 13.2.)

**TABLE 13.2**

# Fund Expenses

|                          | 2013 |
| ------------------------ | ---- |
| Equity funds             | 0.74 |
| Bond funds               | 0.61 |
| Hybrid funds             | 0.80 |
| Money market funds       | 0.17 |
| Target date mutual funds | 0.58 |

*Source:* www.ici.org/pdf/per20-02.pdf.

## Dealing with Medical Student Debt

As previously mentioned, the average debt at graduation for medical students is nearly $180,000. Even though this weighs heavily, most physicians do not doggedly investigate and seek professional advice about dealing with it from advisors who are thoroughly familiar with the remedies. For instance, the Affordable Care Act reduces the income-based repayment formula from 15 percent to 10 percent of adjusted gross income and also reduces the duration of maximum loan repayment from 25 years to 20 years before forgiveness. As a result, physicians can cap their monthly repayments at a reduced rate. If they do not earn a large income over the next 25 years, they may be eligible for loan forgiveness.

The public service option is another option for those with large student debt. The public service loan forgiveness program lets physicians in public service jobs seek loan forgiveness after they've been working for 10 years in a high-need area.

## Not Paying Enough Attention to Asset Protection

Physicians in particular pay attention to professional liability by getting malpractice insurance, but they typically give little thought to nonmedical liability protection against lawsuits by employees or for their actions. Malpractice insurance policies have exclusions or coverage limits, and it's possible to exceed them, which also exposes physicians to liability risk. Putting some assets under a spouse's name may not be enough. It's important to get proper, expert legal advice related to umbrella insurance policies, trusts, or other advanced strategies for high–net–worth individuals.

## Choosing a Bad Financial Advisor

Many healthcare professionals choose a financial advisor during their residency or training. They're busy, so they choose someone by taking the easiest path to an advisor, potentially through a colleague, a friend, or a family member, or sometimes through the local medical society or group. This may be appropriate at the beginning, but when the physician's compensation rapidly increases, the advisor may not be equipped to handle the demands of a family with multiple needs: trusts, taxes, insurance, disability, educational accounts, estate planning, and complex financial planning. Flawed long-term financial strategies combine with an ever-changing tax code to create a big risk over a 30- or 40-year career.

Choosing a financial advisor and tax advisor is one of the most important decisions healthcare professionals make. Most people feel a loyalty to those who helped them in their early years and tend to stick with them, even after it is obvious that the job requires more expertise. Even though physicians are used to dealing with second opinions, they are reluctant to expend a little more time and expense to get another financial opinion. They don't want to seem rude to the first advisor, who is like a pediatrician treating the baby who has grown into an adult. And, of course, the advisor doesn't want to lose a valued client to the competition.

## Not Questioning Financial Advisors Enough

The load/no load distinction is one that medical professionals can read about on many websites and in many books. They are typically more confused by advisors' share class recommendations. With A shares, the load is paid when the investor buys fund shares. With B shares, the charge is paid when the investor sells fund shares. With C shares, the expense is greater but is spread out evenly over the time the investor holds the asset.

It's important to remember that this sales charge is *not* included in the expense ratio. The expense ratio is the fund's operational and administrative cost, divided by the average of the funds' assets. The investor also pays these fees. Even experienced investors find it difficult to accurately determine the fees a commission-based advisor earns.

## Borrowing against Retirement Funds, Which Should Be a Last Resort

Not all qualified plans allow loans; traditional IRAs, Roth IRAs, SEP plans, and SIMPLE IRAs do. People commonly borrow against these funds to pay off a large credit card debt with a high interest rate, to finance education, or to purchase a home. There's no qualification paperwork when you're borrowing from yourself.

Unfortunately, borrowing from these funds keeps that money from compounding and growing, which you count on to build your savings. Furthermore, plans limit how much you can contribute in a given year, so catching up may not be possible. Rules govern the maximum loan amounts. The IRS also has rules about repayment terms, and the loan may be taxable if the borrower doesn't follow the proper schedule. What's more, the borrower pays interest with after-tax dollars and then pays tax on withdrawals in retirement, essentially taxing the money twice.

### Summary

It's possible to avoid all these mistakes with awareness, basic planning, and a little wisdom. Instead of defining success as a huge house, expensive cars, a foreign vacation every year, private schools for children, and more material rewards, medical professionals (and the rest of us) would be smart to pursue peace of mind, a balanced lifestyle, some control over our wants, and an appreciation of the magic of saving and compounding over a long career. Start the financial planning process early. Set goals and review them regularly. Live within your means, manage risk, fund retirement, prioritize insurance, create a rainy-day fund, avoid investments you don't understand, and don't let your desires stand between yourself and financial success.

# CHAPTER 14

# Learning from Professional Athletes' Mistakes

## *Lawrence Funderburke*

Former National Football League player Vince Young earned an estimated $34 million, plus another $30 million in endorsement deals with Reebok, Campbell's Soup, Madden NFL, Vizio, and the National Dairy Council, during his eight years as a professional football player.

In January 2014, Young filed for Chapter 11 bankruptcy in a Houston, Texas, court, after defaulting on a $1.7 million high-interest payday loan. The court ordered many of his personal possessions, including furniture, jewelry, and art, auctioned to pay off his debts.

How did his millions vanish? The answer is a complex collage of lavish spending, bad advice, and trusting the wrong people. Young apparently spent $260,000 a week at the Cheesecake Factory, where he regularly paid for eight teammates to eat and drink. I wonder if he ever thought about buying stock in this publicly traded company, which has doubled in value since his debut and exit from the NFL.

He hosted guests at T.G.I. Friday's, too, spending $6,000 on just one meal. That's a lot of grub! Young bought all the seats on a Southwest Airlines flight from Houston to Nashville in 2007, so he could be the only passenger on the plane and used some of his high-interest loan money to throw himself a pricey birthday party. He had four children with four different women, all in need of support until the kids turn 18.

Growing up with his father in jail, Young may not have learned how to handle money from a childhood role model. The people who should have filled gaps in his financial education may have betrayed him, too. He filed a lawsuit (ultimately settled) against his former agent and his financial planner, alleging that they misappropriated $5.5 million of his money.

## Holes in Their Pockets

It's a sad and all-too-common story. Many professional athletes make a lot more money than they used to, going from an average annual salary of $19,000 in 1960 to a number in the millions today, a sum that's often augmented through apparel and merchandising deals. But only a tiny number of those fortunate, talented few hang on to their wealth when the horn sounds and the game is over. By the time they've been retired for two years, 78 percent of former NFL players are bankrupt, under serious financial stress, or divorced, according to an article in the March 23, 2009, issue of *Sports Illustrated*. Within five years of retirement, 60 percent of former NBA players are out of money.

Even with meaningful academic degrees, it can take former professional athletes four to eight years to adjust to life after sports. When the spotlight fades and the athlete looks for new relevancy, chaos usually ensues, particularly without a bag full of money to smooth the transition. Unfortunately, athletes often fall further and further into a personal and spiritual abyss, leaving behind a trail of broken hearts and shattered dreams. This movie rarely has a happy ending.

Many of those players go from having very little money to making almost unimaginable sums, and it seems to them that they could never spend so much money. So they buy everything they ever wanted: a house for themselves, another for their parents, and perhaps additional properties for friends or girlfriends, all bigger and much more lavish than anyone needs.

Yachts and fancy cars—Hummer, Rolls Royce, Aston Martin—are also popular. When former big league baseball player Jack Clark filed for bankruptcy in July 1992, he owned 18 cars and still owed money on 17 of them. Restaurant bills, bar tabs, and absurd amounts of very expensive alcohol are another big expense. NFL wide receiver Dez Bryant once picked up a $56,000 restaurant tab. Gambling is popular, as is satisfying whimsical personal desires. Mike Tyson had four Bengal tigers. Add in jewelry, gifts, illicit drugs, and tokens designed to impress women, and most players have serious spending problems.

## Inexperience Hurts

They have other problems, too. Most professional athletes are young and too willing to share their newfound wealth; they often lack financial education and may also come from disadvantaged backgrounds. They don't realize that taxes will take a substantial bite of their fat paychecks. They might receive paychecks only during the season but have no idea how to make their cash flow last when it matters even more—in the off-season. The more money you have, the more money you can borrow, so athletes get in trouble with credit cards and other forms of debt, including lines of credit.

Out of a combination of inexperience and loyalty, athletes often hire friends or family members as advisors or financial managers. They blindly trust their parents, siblings, friends, agents, and former coaches. Even when these people aren't trying to skim cash—which they often are—they typically aren't the professionals the athlete's financial situation requires.

Friends and family who don't expect homes or jobs may still aggressively pitch an athlete to invest in their business schemes. All too often, the athletes agree—and generally never see the initial investment or promised return again.

## Learn from Their Mistakes

You may never enjoy the kind of wealth that some young professional athletes earn, but you can still learn a lot from their financial misadventures.

1. **Learn the basics of managing your money**. All too often, professional athletes lack financial savvy. One retired football player

describes cashing his signing-bonus check—at a check-cashing business rather than a bank.

2. **As part of understanding your finances, shop around**. Familiarize yourself with the typical prices of the goods and services you need. Businesses and individuals routinely overcharge professional athletes, just because they can. It's an easy theft, because players often don't know what the normal charge would be.

3. **Invest in stocks, bonds, and other assets**. Some folks feel uneasy in the world of investments, and so they tend to buy tangible assets. That's fine—to a point. A properly diversified portfolio also branches out into the abstract. Just as a team needs players with different skill sets and talents at each position to be successful, a portfolio needs investments that pick up the slack when a teammate underperforms.

4. **Don't ask your child to take care of you**. Too many parents don't plan for their financial futures and hope that their children's talents will pay for college or for the parent's retirement. Sometimes these parents push children into professional sports; I wrote a book many years ago, *Hook Me Up, Playa!*, to dissuade parents from this troubling behavior. Others insist that their kids go into medicine or science. As an adult, you must take responsibility for your own finances, as well as for providing for and protecting the people who depend on you.

5. **Remember that the good times don't last forever**. A professional athlete might have between three and five years at his maximum lifetime income. People in other lines of work typically have greater longevity, of course, but you'll probably have some jobs that pay better than others through the course of your career. When you're earning more, you'll be tempted to buy all the things you wanted, but couldn't afford when you were earning less. Enjoy some of your money, but also take the opportunity to save and invest money when you have it.

When I was playing professional basketball, I put away 50 percent of my paycheck every two weeks. I knew that my personal money ball would eventually stop bouncing. When that day inevitably came, I would need a financial cushion to help me reach my next adventure, which wouldn't involve sports. The average person should invest or save at least 10 percent from each paycheck in order to fund 80 percent of current lifestyle expenses in retirement. (Of course, this still leaves a shortfall of 20 percent.) To achieve financial freedom, an individual or couple should set aside 30 percent of take-home pay to fund retirement goals.

6.  **Athletes often hire the wrong people and trust them far too much, putting family and friends on the payroll or trusting an agent or former coach to do things that are far outside their areas of expertise**. Don't hire a financial advisor, lawyer, accountant, stockbroker, estate planner, or other financial professional because you're related or because you're friends. Hire professionals because they have the qualifications and credentials they need to do the work you need them to do.

    It's possible that your father is the best divorce lawyer or that your high school buddy is a good accountant. If the relationship is there, that's great. But don't give the business to someone who isn't qualified, just because you want to be nice. And no matter whom you hire, pay attention to the work being done on your behalf. Don't worry about hurting someone's feelings by probing their decision-making abilities. A competent professional has nothing to hide and will welcome your inquiries.

7.  **Remember that you're not an expert in everything**. Maybe you're very good at your job and also play a mean game of tennis. That doesn't mean you'll unerringly pick good private equity deals or other investments. Hire people who know more than you do about areas that aren't your strongest suits. Don't ever commit to an investment deal without first carefully weighing the pros and cons.

Glamorous-sounding deals are often glitzy attempts to separate you from your money. If it sounds too good to be true, it probably is.

8. **Say no**. This saved me a lot of heartache and grief as a professional athlete, because I set boundaries on my giving. If you're doing well financially and your friends or family are not, there's a good chance that they'll ask or expect you to pick up the tab when you go out, lend or give them money, or invest in their business ventures. If you're like many professional athletes, you'll try to be the hero. It's fine to take a friend out to lunch when you can afford to do so, of course, but don't make the mistake of thinking that you can save people from their own financial problems. You can't. You didn't cause their problems and you shouldn't feel obligated to fix them. Don't throw money away by trying. Financial salvation only comes when a person's insatiable appetites and competitive desires are placed on the altar.

9. **Approach marriage and family in a serious frame of mind**. By conservative, common estimates among athletes and agents, the divorce rate for professional athletes ranges from 60 percent to 80 percent. Divorce, with its ability to split wealth in half and usher in years of alimony and child support payments, can be financially disastrous. Do your best to avoid it.

    Of course, a prenuptial agreement can soften the blow. Consult a family law attorney if you need or want such an agreement. My wife, Monya, and I do not have a prenuptial agreement. Neither of us wanted the option of divorce hanging over our heads.

10. **Ignore the Joneses**. Professional athletes are competitive people, and they compete with one another to see who can have the coolest toys. Stay out of that contest. Live below your means. People achieve financial freedom when they live 30 percent below take-home pay, though I realize this is a tall order for anyone who works to make ends meet on a typical salary. Buy the things that you want and can afford, not the things that you think will

help you keep pace with the neighbors. While I was in the NBA, I knew that I couldn't afford to keep up with my better-paid teammates, a group that included Chris Webber and Vlade Divac. I never even tried, which served me and my family well.

Last but certainly not least, develop a sense of who you are outside of your work and the money it earns. What are your goals? Your beliefs? What nonnegotiable things do you value in life? What gives your life purpose and meaning? If you never know who you are at your core, you're in trouble. If you do know, however, you're much more likely to keep your financial life on an even keel and respond appropriately when changing circumstances threaten to upset your boat.

In 99 percent of the cases of financial distress I see, the problem is a disconnect between stated values and spending habits. Without a real value system, spending habits become your default value system. A personally bankrupt life, which is an out-of-control and reckless existence, almost always precedes financial bankruptcy when the discussion involves pro athletes.

After all the financial turmoil he endured, Vince Young's movie reel has a new twist. In 2015, he began volunteering for the Austin Sunshine Club, where he mentors kids, helping them get the tools they'll need to overcome life's challenges. It's a great way to turn his mistakes into wisdom for the next generation. Personal experience is often the best teacher, particularly the kind involving monetary turnovers. I'm sure Young would agree.

# About the Contributors

**Stephen A. Lukan** is a certified, fee-only financial planner with John E. Sestina and Company. Lukan graduated from The Pennsylvania State University in 1994 and has been in practice for 14 years, serving clients throughout the United States. In addition to helping his clients with their comprehensive planning needs, Lukan was elected to the National Association of Personal Financial Advisors (NAPFA)'s Midwest regional board in 2015 and is entering his sixth year as co-host of the weekly financial planning radio show *Managing to Be Wealthy* on 610 WTVN. Outside the office, Lukan volunteered as his condo association president for five years. He enjoys football and ice hockey, and lives in Dublin, Ohio, with his wife, Alison.

**Tyler V. Cook** is a certified, fee-only financial planner and a senior financial planner with John E. Sestina and Company. A member of the Sestina Network of Fee-Only Financial Planners since 2006, Cook lives in Dublin, Ohio.

**Lawrence Funderburke** is perhaps best known for his exploits on the basketball court at The Ohio State University and in the NBA, but his heart has always gravitated to financial management, wealth building, and philanthropic pursuits. A dean's list student and magna cum laude business finance graduate at Ohio State, Funderburke is also passionate about motivating and educating young people and adults in financial life skills—a must-have for our dynamic twenty-first century. He and his wife, Monya, run LFYO.org, a 501(c)3 nonprofit that empowers economically challenged youth and families. They recently started a for-profit business, FunderMax Fitness, a health and wealth studio for youth, adults, and families (www.FunderMaxFitness.com).

**Kimberly E. Wirtz** is a certified financial planner who works from her home in Strongsville, Ohio. She has been with John E. Sestina and Company for 11 years. Wirtz has three children and in her spare time coaches middle school volleyball. She is a member of both the Financial Planning Association and NAPFA. An avid golfer, Wirtz is also the president of the Columbia Hills Womens' Golf Association.

**Bhagwan Satiani**, MD, MBA, FACS, FACHE, is professor of clinical surgery in the division of vascular diseases and surgery, medical director of the Non-Invasive Vascular Laboratory, and director of the Faculty Leadership Institute, all at Wexner Medical Center at The Ohio State University College of Medicine in Columbus, Ohio. He also serves as president of Savvy Medicine, a business of medicine education company, and as commissioner of Ohio's minority health commission. His published books include *The Smarter Physician* series, *The Coming Shortage of Surgeons: Why They Are Disappearing and What We Can Do About It*, *An American Journey: Life Lessons for Parents of Immigrant Children*, and *Color Atlas & Synopsis of Vascular Diseases*.

Satiani volunteers for ASHA-Ray of Hope, a Columbus, Ohio, organization that works to prevent domestic violence in the South Asian community. He plays percussion for the Indian music group Jhankar.

# About the Author

**W**idely acknowledged as the "father of fee-only financial planning," John E. Sestina is president of John E. Sestina and Company, a private professional financial planning firm that counsels individual clients on an objective, fee-only basis. The firm's guidance to clients throughout North America includes cash flow management, investment management, tax planning, disability planning, education planning, retirement planning, and estate planning.

Sestina has met the qualifications for the professional designations of Certified Financial Planner (CFP) and Chartered Financial Consultant (ChFC). He earned a bachelor of science degree from the University of Dayton in Dayton, Ohio and a master of science in financial services from The American College in Bryn Mawr, Pennsylvania.

Since 1972, Sestina has been recognized as the founder of the profession of fee-only financial planning. His record of visionary innovation has supported his mission to establish fee-only financial planning as an independent profession. His stature as the founding leader in his profession is reflected in a long career of firsts and noteworthy achievements in financial planning education and service. Sestina is the author of the only book on the market that outlines a step-by-step guide to help individual consumers prepare their own financial plan.

He also shares 50 years of successful private practice experience with his profession through *Fee-Only Financial Planning: How to Make It Work for You* (Dearborn, 1991), the leading book in its field. In order to promote professionalism and credibility in a then-fledgling field, Mr. Sestina founded two fee-only professional associations: the Society of Independent Financial Advisors (SIFA) in 1976 and the National Association of Personal Financial Advisors (NAPFA) in 1982.

Sestina was awarded the coveted Robert J. Underwood lifetime service award by the National Association of Personal Financial Advisors in

2008. He has been named one of the nation's best financial advisors in every year since *WORTH* magazine began its rigorous, in-depth annual research process in 1996. *Medical Economics* also honored Sestina in its "Best 120 Financial Advisers for Doctors" (August 1998).

Nationally recognized as a leader and innovator, he is often quoted in such national media as the *Wall Street Journal*, the *New York Times*, *Kiplinger's Personal Finance*, *USA Today*, *Newsweek*, *U.S. News & World Report*, and *Bloomberg Business News*. In 2011, he began working with 610 WTVN radio, hosting the first financial planning show on radio, *Managing to Be Wealthy*.

# Index